Discover
ENGLISH
Workbook

2

with CD-ROM

IZABELLA HEARN

Pearson Education Limited
Edinburgh Gate
Harlow
Essex CM20 2JE
England
and Associated Companies throughout the world.

www.pearsonelt.com

First published 2010
Fourteenth impression 2021

ISBN 978-1-4082-0936-3

Set in 12/15pt ATQuay Sans Book, 12/15pt ATQuay Medium,
9/11pt Helvetica Condensed Medium and 9/11pt Helvetica Neue
Medium Condensed.

Printed and bound by CPI Group (UK) Ltd, Croydon, CR0 4YY

Acknowledgements

Illustrated by Sean Longcroft, Andy Peters, Melanie Sharp,
Tony Wilkins and Eric Smith.

The publisher would like to thank the following for their kind
permission to reproduce their photographs:

(Key: b-bottom; c-centre; l-left; r-right; t-top)

Alamy Images: AA World Travel Library 46r, Anthony Hatley 63/2,
INSADCO Photography 26, JupiterImages/Ablestock 55/1, Kuttig -
People 14/2, Music Alan King 55/7, Robert Harding Picture Library
Ltd 39/5, Alex Segre 32, Steve Bloom Images 39/3; **Art Directors
and TRIP photo Library:** Chris Kapolka 39/8, Constance Toms
63/5; **Children of Uganda:** www.childrenofuganda.org 62t, 62b;
Corbis: Theo Allofs 39/4, EPA 11, Eurasia Press/Steven Vidler 39/6,
Blaine Harrington III 39/7, Eduardo Longoni 39/1, MAPS.com 65;
DK Images: 55/3, Peter Chadwick 55/5, Nigel Hicks 39/2, Chris
Stowers 34t; **Getty Images:** Dorling Kindersley 55/4, 55/8, LWA
19, Patti McConville 72; **Don Hooper:** Photographers Direct 63/4;
Kobal Collection Ltd: Tiger Aspect Pics/Giles Keyte 73; **Lonely
Planet Images:** Ann Cecil 41; **Martin Beddall:** 2tl, 2tr, 2br, 3/1,
3/2, 3/3, 3/4, 4, 5t, 9 (Katie), 9 (Ravi), 9t, 9b, 25, 46l, 50, 51, 56,
57l, 57c, 57r, 58tl, 58tr, 63b, 64, 81t; **Photolibrary.com:** Stockbyte
14/1; **PunchStock:** BananaStock 14tr, 59; **Reuters:** Guillermo Granja
76; **Rex Features:** Anglia Press Agency Ltd 5b, Denis Closon 63/1,
Everett/Columbia 81b, David Hartley 43, Image Source 55/2, 55/6,
55/9, Steve Lyne 14/3, Brian Rasic 58bl, Shout 63/3, Kim Woods
49; **Thinkstock:** Thinkstock Images 14/4; **www.PerfectPhoto.CA/©
Rob vanNostrand:** 34b

All other images © Pearson Education

Every effort has been made to trace the copyright holders and we
apologise in advance for any unintentional omissions. We would
be pleased to insert the appropriate acknowledgement in any
subsequent edition of this publication.

Join Discovery Web!

My Picture Dictionary

Objects and body parts

1 Circle six words.

magazinelizardT-shirtwatchdrinkjacket

2 Label the photos with the words in Exercise 1.

1 *magazine*

2 _____

3 _____

4 _____

5 _____

6 _____

3 Circle the body parts and label the photos.

mouthnoseeyesearshair

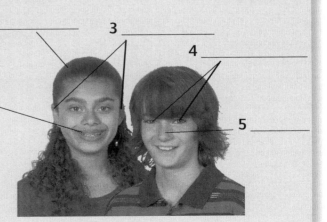

1 *mouth*

2 _____

3 _____

4 _____

5 _____

to be / have got

4 ☆ Read page 4 of the Students' Book again. True or false? Write the sentences in full. Correct the false sentences.

1 Ravi's got a pet. **_true_**
  Ravi has got a pet.
2 His name's Yoda. _____
  _____
3 Yoda's a dog. _____
  _____
4 He's clever. _____
  _____
5 He's got six legs. _____
  _____
6 He's got big ears. _____
  _____

5 ☆☆ Complete the sentences with the correct form of the verbs in brackets.

1 Ravi _is_ (be) eleven. ✔
2 He _____ (have got) a dog. ✗
3 He _____ (be) Ben's brother. ✗
4 Ravi and Ben _____ (be) friends. ✔
5 Katie _____ (have got) a lizard. ✗
6 Monica _____ (have got) a dog. ✔
7 We _____ (be) in their class. ✗
8 I _____ (have got) a pet. ✔

6 ☆ Complete the questions. Use _is, are, has_ or _have_. Match the questions with the answers.

1 How old _is_ she?
2 _____ she got a pet lizard?
3 _____ Monica and Ben her friends?
4 _____ they got a website?
a Yes, they are.
b No, she hasn't.
c Yes, they have.
d She's eleven.

1 _d_ 2 ____ 3 ____ 4 ____

7 ☆☆ What have they got? Follow the lines and write sentences.

1

Ravi

2

Monica

3

Katie

4

Monica and Ben

saxophone

mobile phone

website

lizard

1 _Ravi has got a lizard._
2 _____
3 _____
4 _____

8 ☆☆ Complete the sentences for you.

1 I _____ (be) twelve.
2 I _____ (have got) a pet.
3 I _____ (have got) a sister.
4 I _____ (be) small.
5 I _____ (have got) a _____.
6 I _____ (be) _____.

Meet The Team!

Computer words

1 Find the computer words.

1 [M] [T] [A] [O] [U] [M] [S] [E]

   mouse mat

2 [S] [E] [N] [R] [E] [C]

   _____

3 [R] [N] [T] [E] [P] [R] [I]

   _____

4 [Y] [B] [D] [O] [E] [K] [A] [R]

   _____

5 [P] [K] [S] [S] [R] [A] [E] [E]

   _____

Years

2 Write the years in numbers. Use these numbers.

| 2001   1987   2016   1806   ~~1898~~   1990 |

1 eighteen ninety-eight = ***1898***
2 nineteen ninety = _____
3 nineteen eighty-seven = _____
4 two thousand and one = _____
5 eighteen oh six = _____
6 twenty sixteen = _____

3 Write the years in words.

1 1898 = *eighteen ninety-eight*
2 1968 = _____
3 2011 = _____
4 2001 = _____
5 1980 = _____
6 1887 = _____

can

4 ☆ Match the words.

1 climb   a a picture
2 sing   b photos
3 read   c a song
4 paint   d walls
5 take   e books

5 ☆ Look at the table. Complete the sentences.

	climb walls	take photos	dance	swim
Ravi	✗	✔	✗	✔
Yoda	✔	✗	✗	✔

1 Ravi can swim and ***take photos*** but he can't
   _____ or _____ .
2 Yoda can _____ too, but he can't
   _____ or _____ .

6 ☆ Read the text and answer the questions. Use *Yes, she can.* or *No, she can't.*

Hi!
Can you use a keyboard? I can and Koko can too. Koko is a gorilla from California. She can do a lot of things. She can chat on the computer and she can make jokes. She can't write songs and she can't play the guitar, but she can paint. She's very clever!

1 Can Monica use a keyboard? ***Yes, she can.***
2 Can Koko do a lot of things? _____
3 Can Koko write songs?_____
4 Can Koko paint? _____
5 Can Koko play the guitar? _____

7 ☆☆ Order the words.

1 can Koko What do
   What can Koko do?
2 is old she How
   _____?
3 Can English speak she
   _____?
4 blue eyes got Has she
   _____?
5 she Can paint
   _____?

8 ☆ Match the questions from Exercise 7 with the answers. Write the numbers.

1   a She can do a lot of things.
_____ b No, she hasn't got blue eyes.
_____ c Yes, she can paint.
_____ d No, she can't speak English.
_____ e She's thirty-eight.

9 Read the text in Exercise 6 again. Circle the correct answers.

Name:	(Koko) / Kiko
Year of birth:	1831 / 1972
Hobby:	painting / rollerblading
She can:	play the saxophone / use a keyboard

10 Complete the profiles for you and a friend.

Name:	
Date of birth:	
Hobby:	
I can:	

Name:	
Date of birth:	
Hobby:	
He / She can:	

Starter B

5

Adventure Island

1 Follow the lines. Write sentences.

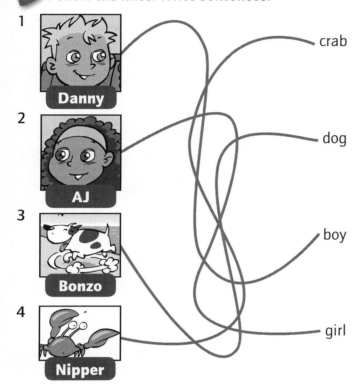

1 *Danny is a boy.*
2 _____
3 _____
4 _____

2 Complete the text. Use these words.

> name   likes   ~~island~~   crab   Nipper   dog
> happy   favourite

Danny and AJ are on an ¹ *island*. Danny's got a
² _____ . The dog's ³ _____ is Bonzo. There's a
⁴ _____ on the island. The crab's name is
⁵ _____ . AJ isn't ⁶ _____ . Crabs aren't her
⁷ _____ animals, but she ⁸ _____ Bonzo.

Imperatives

3 ⭐ Find the imperatives.

1 a d t S n p u   *Stand up*!
2 k o L o   _____ !
3 o e C m e e h r   _____ !
4 o n D ' t l a t k   _____ !

Nipper's Learning Blog

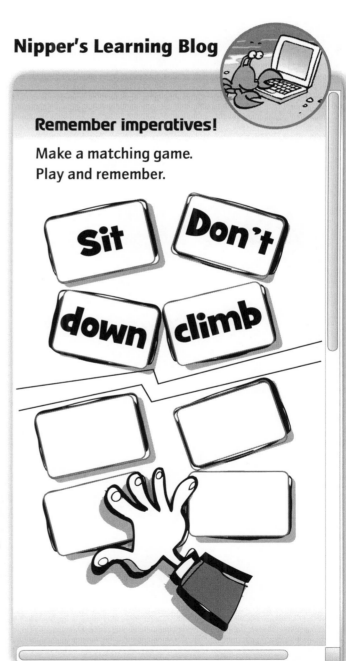

Remember imperatives!

Make a matching game.
Play and remember.

My Picture Dictionary

Free time activities

1 Complete the words.

① s _i_ ng in a
b _a_ _n_ _d_

② m__ __ __
jewe__ __ __ __ __

③ d__ __ __
cart__ __ __ __

④ pl__ __ b__ __ __d
__ __mes

⑤ t__ __ __
fr__ __ __ __ __

⑥ r__ __d
b__ __ __s

⑦ __oll__ __ __
__ __rds

⑧ m__ __ __
mo__ __ __ __lanes

⑨ li__ __ __ __ to
__ __ __ r__ __ __ __

⑩ g__ roll__ __bladi__ __

2 What is your favourite free time activity?

_____

3 Order the activities in Exercise 1 for you. Your favourite
activity is 1, the activity you like least is 10.

my words

Do you know more free
time activities?
Write them here.

_____

_____

_____

Discover **5** extra words. Go to page 87.

Talking Tips!

1 Write sentences. Use these words.

> impossible   down   that's   slow

1 _____

2 _____

Present simple

2 ⭐ Follow the lines. Complete the sentences about what Sue does every day.

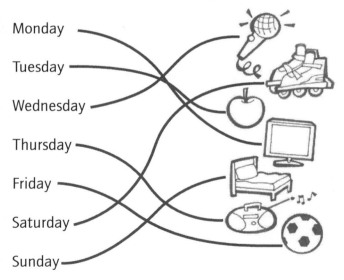

Monday
Tuesday
Wednesday
Thursday
Friday
Saturday
Sunday

1 Sue **_watches_** (watch) **_TV_** on Mondays.
2 Sue _____ (eat) _____ on _____ .
3 Sue _____ (sing) _____ on _____ .
4 Sue _____ (listen) _____ on Thursdays.
5 Sue _____ (play) _____ on _____ .
6 Sue _____ (go) _____ on Saturdays.
7 Sue _____ (stay) _____ on Sundays.

3 ⭐⭐ Write sentences. Use the present simple.

1 Ben / read magazines / Sundays ✓
   Ben reads magazines on Sundays.
2 Katie / go rollerblading / Saturdays ✗
   _____
3 We / watch TV / Sunday mornings ✗
   _____
4 Ben / do homework / Saturday evenings ✓
   _____
5 I / listen to music / Fridays ✓
   _____
6 They / go climbing / Thursdays ✗
   _____

Frequency adverbs

4 ⭐ Find five frequency adverbs in the word square.

L	E	T	A	S	G	O	R	O
U	S	U	A	L	L	Y	O	F
L	L	E	R	B	W	L	A	T
D	N	E	V	E	R	A	I	E
N	G	T	O	D	A	Y	Y	N
S	O	M	E	T	I	M	E	S

5 Write the letters from the word square that are not adverbs. Complete the sentence.

L _ _' _ _ _
_ _ _ _ _ _ _ _ _ _ _
_ _ _ _ _ .

6 ☆ Look at the table. Complete the sentences.

At the weekend

	draws cartoons	plays board games	plays football	takes photos
Monica	00	00000	00	X
Ravi	00	00	X	000
Katie	00	00000	X	000
Ben	X	000	00000	000

00000 = always	000 = often
00 = sometimes	X = never

1 Monica ***always*** plays board games.
2 Ravi _____ plays football.
3 Katie _____ draws cartoons.
4 Ben _____ takes photos.

7 ☆ Look at the table again. Read the dialogues. Who answers the questions?

1
A What do you do at the weekend?
B I often play board games but I never draw cartoons.
   Ben

2
A What do you do at the weekend?
B I often take photos and sometimes I draw cartoons or play board games.
   _____

3
A What do you do at the weekend?
B Sometimes I draw cartoons and I often take photos but I always play board games.
   _____

4
A What do you do at the weekend?
B I never take photos but I sometimes draw cartoons.
   _____

8 ☆☆ Order the words.

1 | often | sing | do | How | you |
   How often do you sing?
2 | When | to | listen | you | do | music |
   _____?
3 | do | often | make | you | jewellery | How |
   _____?
4 | watch | you | TV | When | do |
   _____?
5 | usually | you | do | Where | study |
   _____?

9 ☆☆☆ Write your answers to the questions in Exercise 8.

1 _____
2 _____
3 _____
4 _____
5 _____

TV programmes

1 Label the programmes. Use these words.

> a cartoon   the news   a quiz show
> a series   a sports programme
> a wildlife show

a cartoon _____ _____

_____ _____ _____

2 Complete the days of the week.

	10 a.m.	11.00 a.m.	1.30 p.m.	3 p.m.
M _o_ _n_ _d_ _a_ _y_	News	Super Quiz	Animals of Africa	Sports Time
Tu__ __ __ __ __	News	Cartoons	News	Sports Time
Wed__ __ __ __ __ __	News	Super Quiz	Cartoons	The Robinsons
Th__ __ __ __ __ __	News	Super Quiz	The Robinsons	Sports Time
F__ __ __ __ __	News	Cartoons	Animal Life	Sports Time
Sa__ __ __ __ __ __	News	Super Quiz	Sports Time	Sports Time
Su__ __ __ __	News	Animal Life	Cartoons	The Robinsons

3 Read the TV magazine in Exercise 2. True or false?

1 The news is on every day.
   true
2 The quiz show is usually on in the morning. _____
3 The wildlife programme is never on Mondays. _____
4 The series _The Robinsons_ is sometimes on at three o'clock. _____
5 The sports programme is often on in the afternoon. _____
6 The cartoons are never on in the afternoon. _____

Present continuous

4 ☆ Complete the table.

verb	present continuous
talk	talking
¹ _**wear**_	wearing
win	² _____
³ _____	carrying
throw	⁴ _____

5 ⭐⭐ Complete the sports report. Use words from Exercise 4.

Water Sports Special

Good evening! We are ¹ _talking_ to you today from the Underwater Football Game in Bangkok. There are eleven players in a team and every player is ² _____ red or green. The players today are all men. Wow! A player in red is ³ _____ the ball into the goal! The red team has got the ball again! They are ⁴ _____ it to the goal. Yes! The ball is in the goal! Goal! The red team is ⁵ _____ .

6 ⭐ Change these questions to the present continuous.

1 Where does the programme come from?
**Where is the programme coming from**?

2 What do the teams wear?
_____?

3 What does the player in red do?
_____?

4 What do the red team do?
_____?

5 Who wins the game?
_____?

7 ⭐⭐ Now answer the questions in Exercise 6.

1 _____
2 _____
3 _____
4 _____
5 _____

8 ⭐⭐⭐ Imagine you are watching your favourite TV show now. What is happening? Write sentences.

_____
_____
_____
_____
_____
_____
_____
_____
_____
_____
_____
_____
_____

Present simple and present continuous

1 ⭐⭐ Order the words. Then underline the present simple and circle the present continuous.

1 | at | wear | I | a | uniform | school |
I wear a uniform at school.

2 | wearing | I | shorts | am |
_____

3 | at | hamburgers | lunchtime | eat | I |
_____

4 | fish | eating | am | I |
_____

5 | sport | we | play | school | after |
_____

6 | with | Bonzo | we | playing | are |
_____

2 ⭐⭐ Look at your answers for Exercise 1. Add *every day* or *at the moment*.

3 ⭐⭐ Complete the sentences with the verbs in brackets. Use the present simple or present continuous.

1 She **makes** (make) jewellery at the weekend.
2 We _____ (play) board games at the moment.
3 They _____ (win) every match.
4 At lunchtime I _____ (stop) work.
5 He _____ (help) his friends now.
6 You _____ (wear) new trousers today.
7 You _____ (cook) the lunch every day.

4 ⭐ Make the sentences in Exercise 3 negative. Use *doesn't*, *don't*, *isn't* or *aren't*.

1 _She doesn't make jewellery at the weekend._
2 _____
3 _____
4 _____
5 _____
6 _____
7 _____

5 ⭐ Read AJ's diary. Complete the questions with these words. Write two more questions.

Are   Do   Does   Is   Do

Danny's cooking breakfast. He often cooks. I'm not helping him. I never help with the food.

It's very hot. Nipper and Bonzo are sleeping. I'm not feeling very well today.

I like the evenings. We sometimes watch the sea and talk. It's good.

1 _Does_ Danny often cook the breakfast?
2 _____ AJ helping him?
3 _____ Nipper and Bonzo sleeping?
4 _____ they play music in the evenings?
5 _____ they watch the sea?
6 _____?
7 _____?

6 ⭐⭐ Answer the questions in Exercise 5.

1 *Yes, he does.*

2 _____

3 _____

4 _____

5 _____

6 _____

7 _____

7 Order the sentences.

Bonzo's Dream

☐ Then he has an idea!

☐ They are looking for shells.

☐ Now, Nipper is helping them with the jewellery too!

[1] Bonzo is helping AJ with her jewellery.

8 Complete Bonzo's poem. Use these words.

Do   are   ~~every~~   getting

Bonzo's Notes

Fish ¹ ___*every*___ day!
They ² _____ all ³ _____ fat.
But fish isn't good!
⁴ _____ they think I'm a cat?

9 Read the poem in Exercise 8 again and answer the questions.

1 Do they often eat fish? _____

2 Does Bonzo like fish? _____

3 Do cats eat fish? _____

Nipper's Learning Blog

Make a diary for every week.

Write the days of the week.

Write the activities that you do every day.

Monday

play football

Tuesday

go climbing

Reading

1 Read the letter. Underline a sentence to match each of the four photos.

Hi! I'm Jan and I'm from the Netherlands. I go to school every day but after school I usually go to a club with my friends. At the club we do different activities in small groups. There are ten children in my group. We come from different countries but we all speak English.
Sometimes we play football. We play table tennis too. We can do painting too. It's fun! Today is Friday. We're learning how to make jewellery. I'm making a present for my sister. It's her birthday tomorrow. My friends are making masks for a show. Their parents are helping. We all love the club!

2 Answer the questions.

1 Where does Jan usually go after school?

   He usually goes to a club.

2 Where are the children from?

   _____

3 What language do they all speak?

   _____

4 What's Jan doing now?

   _____

5 What are his friends doing now?

   _____

6 Who is helping them?

   _____

Writing

3 Write about your perfect club.
- What activities can you do?
- Can you go every day?
- How many children are in the club?
- Can you play sports?
- What different things can you make?

_____

_____

_____

_____

_____

_____

_____

_____

2 I'm Hungry!

My Picture Dictionary

Food

1 Complete the words. Label the pictures.

 ① _e_ ggs

 ② str__wb__rr____s

 ③ cr__sps

 ④ c__rr__ts

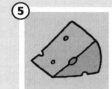 ⑤ ch____s__

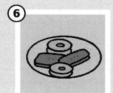 ⑥ b__sc____ts

 ⑦ b__n__n__s

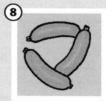 ⑧ s____s__g__s

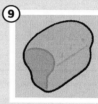 ⑨ br____d

 ⑩ m____t

 ⑪ f__zzy dr__nk

 ⑫ b____ns

 ⑬ __n____n

 ⑭ p__t__t_____

2 Find and write the food words.

1 a glass of _water_
2 a bowl of _____
3 a bag of _____
4 a can of _____
5 a plate of _____

   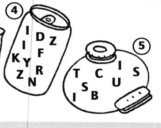

3 Complete the lists for you. Use food words.

I like:

1 _____
2 _____
3 _____

I don't like:

1 _____
2 _____
3 _____

my words

Do you know more food words? Write them here.

_____
_____
_____

Discover **5** extra words. Go to page 87.

1 Circle the healthy food and drink.

crisps   water   rice   carrots   chocolate
fizzy drink   fish   salad   biscuits   fruit

Talking Tips!

2 Complete the posters with these words. Draw pictures on the posters.

IT'S   FOR   DELICIOUS   YOU   GOOD   VERY   IT'S

① **Vegetable Stir-fry**

IT'S _____

_____

② **Fruit Smoothie**

_____

_____

Countable and uncountable nouns

3 ☆ Complete the shopping lists. Use these words.

bread   potato   meat   biscuit   water   rice
sausage   onion   chocolate   egg

countable   uncountable

an onion
_____
_____
_____

rice
_____
_____
_____

some and *any*

4 ⭐ **Complete the text. Use *some* or *any*. Look at the pictures and write the names of the rats.**

Rick, Ron and Rowena have all got ¹ _**some**_ crisps and ² _____ bread. They haven't got ³ _____ fish. Reg and Rick have got an apple and ⁴ _____ strawberries. Ron hasn't got ⁵ _____ fruit but he's got ⁶ _____ cheese and a can of beans. Rowena hasn't got ⁷ _____ cheese but she's got a sausage and ⁸ _____ biscuits.

1 _____

2 _____

3 _____

4 _____

5 ⭐⭐ **Order the words.**

1 Rowena | got | beans | Has | any
Has Rowena got any beans _____ ?

2 fruit | Ron | got | any | Has
_____ ?

3 Reg | Has | any | strawberries | got
_____ ?

4 any | Rick | and | got | chocolate | Ron | Have
_____ ?

5 and | any | Have | Reg | Rick | cheese | got
_____ ?

6 ⭐ **Look at Exercise 4. Write answers to the questions in Exercise 5.**

1 _No, she hasn't._
2 _____
3 _____
4 _____
5 _____

7 ⭐⭐⭐ **Complete the sentences for you. Remember to use plurals for countable words.**

I often eat _____
_____

I never eat _____
_____

8 ⭐ **Look at Katie's lunchbox. True or false?**

1 Katie's got an apple.   _true_
2 She's got some bread.   _____
3 She's got some rice.   _____
4 She hasn't got any cheese.   _____
5 She's got an egg.   _____
6 She's got some strawberries.   _____

9 ⭐⭐⭐ **Imagine this is your lunchbox. Write six sentences.**

1 I've got some _____
2 I haven't got any _____
3 _____
4 _____
5 _____
6 _____

Don't Do This At Home!

Monica's fridge

Ravi's fridge

1 **Look at the two fridges. True or false?**

1 Monica drinks a lot of fizzy drinks. _____true_____

2 Monica doesn't eat much chocolate. _____

3 Ravi eats a lot of sausages. _____

4 Ravi doesn't eat any cheese. _____

much / many / a lot of

2 ⭐⭐ **Write six sentences. Use *much*, *many* or *a lot of*.**

Monica's fridge
There isn't much fruit.
_____
_____
_____

Ravi's fridge
There's a lot of rice.
_____
_____
_____

3 ⭐ Look at the Colossus family's shopping list. Complete the sentences. Use *much*, *many*, *any* or *a lot of*.

eggs	144	
carrots	0	
rice	1	bag
meat	2	packets
cheese	15	packets
bananas	26	
water	2	bottles
fizzy drinks	4	cans
biscuits	1	packet

1 They don't eat **much** rice.
2 They don't eat _____ carrots.
3 They eat _____ eggs.
4 They don't drink _____ fizzy drinks.
5 They don't drink _____ water.
6 They don't eat _____ rice.

4 ⭐⭐ Read Mrs Colossus's answers. Write the questions.

1 How many **eggs do you eat**?
We eat a lot of eggs.
2 How much _____?
We don't drink much water.
3 _____?
We don't eat many biscuits.
4 _____?
We eat a lot of bananas.
5 _____?
We don't eat much meat.

5 ⭐⭐⭐ What does your family eat and drink? Write sentences.

1 We eat a lot of _____
_____
2 We don't _____
_____
3 _____
_____
4 _____
_____

6 Read and circle the answer.

Does your family have a healthy diet?
Yes, we do. / No, we don't.

7 ⭐ Complete the poem. Use *How much* or *How many*.

1 _____ potatoes?
2 _____ cheese?
3 _____ sausages?
Sixteen please!
4 _____ eggs?
5 _____ rice?
6 _____ chocolate?
Chocolate's nice!

Adventure Island

1 Find these words in the word square. Write the extra letters.

bread bean egg crab juice
coconut onion meat

C	R	A	B	C	B
O	D	H	E	M	R
C	N	S	A	E	E
O	E	I	N	A	A
N	I	G	O	T	D
U	A	W	G	N	N
T	J	U	I	C	E

Extra letters: _____

2 Reorder the extra letters from Exercise 1 to complete the sentence.

Nipper likes insects in his _____ .

3 Circle the correct words. Look and tick the correct picture.

There isn't ¹ **a lot of / many** food today. There aren't ² **much / many** bananas and there isn't ³ **much / many** juice. There aren't ⁴ **many / much** biscuits and there isn't ⁵ **many / much** salad. There's ⁶ **a lot of / much** fish and there are ⁷ **much / a lot of** crabs' legs. Yuk!

Ⓐ   Ⓑ

4 Complete the questions. Look at the table and write the answers. What do they eat in a week?

	bananas	crabs	juice
Nipper	6	X	3 bowls
Bonzo	15	21	X

1 How **_much_** juice **_do you drink_**?
   I drink **_three bowls of juice_**.
2 How _____ crabs _____?
   I don't eat any crabs!
3 How many _____?
   I eat _____.

4 How **_much_** juice **_do you drink_**?
   _____.
5 _____ crabs _____?
   Yum! I eat a lot of crabs!
6 How _____?
   _____.

20

Offers and requests

5 This dialogue is mixed up! Write it again in the correct order.

Of course. Here you are.
Yes, please. Can I have a biscuit too, please?
Yuk! That's disgusting!
Oh no! There are insects on the plate!
Mmm! The juice is delicious!
Would you like some juice?

A *Would you like some juice?*
B _____
A _____
B _____
A _____
B _____

6 Order the words.

1 hotdog you Would like Bonzo a
_____?

2 you juice Would some AJ like insect
_____?

3 a Would like you Danny coconut
_____?

7 Find the answers to the questions in Exercise 6 in the spiral.

nothankyouyukthat'sdisgustingmmmdelicious

1 _____
2 _____
3 _____

8 Separate the words of Bonzo's poem.

Bonzo's Notes

Thereisn'tmuchfoodhere.
There isn't much food here.
It'sadog'slife,man!
_____
Iwouldloveasausage,
_____
Orsomemeatinacan.
_____
Wouldyoulikeacoconut?
_____
Afishoracrab?
_____
There'snotalottoeat.
_____
Thisisallwehave.
_____

9 Circle the five food words in Bonzo's Notes.

Nipper's Learning Blog

Remember words!

To remember words, draw them. Draw some food on this table. Then label it.

Let's Revise!

2d

Vocabulary

1 Find the food words.

1 b e s a t l g e v e _____
2 s i h f   _____
3 o r t a r c   _____
4 w i s a d n c h _____
5 m a t e   _____
6 a e n b s   _____

2 Circle the correct words.

1 a packet of **bread** / **biscuits**
2 a bottle of **water** / **eggs**
3 a plate of **fizzy drink** / **sausages**
4 a glass of **crisps** / **juice**
5 a bowl of **rice** / **sandwich**
6 a can of **salad** / **fizzy drink**

___/12

Grammar

3 Write *a*, *an* or *some*.

1 _____ onion
2 _____ water
3 _____ sugar
4 _____ rice
5 _____ banana

4 Complete the sentences. Use *much*, *many* or *a lot of*.

1 I'm hungry! There isn't _____ cheese on this pizza.
2 There aren't _____ sandwiches on the plate.
3 There isn't _____ juice!
4 Great! There are _____ biscuits.
5 There is _____ ice cream too.

5 Look at the picture of a smoothie. Complete the questions and answers.

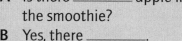

1
A Are there _____ bananas in the smoothie?
B No, there aren't _____ bananas.

2
A Is there _____ apple in the smoothie?
B Yes, there _____.

3
A Is there a _____ in the smoothie?
B No, there _____ a carrot.

4
A Are there _____ strawberries in the smoothie?
B Yes, there _____.

___/18

Functions

6 Complete the words.

Ben   ¹ W__ __ld you ² l__k__ a biscuit?
Monica No, thank you. ³ C__n you ⁴ p__ss the fruit, please?
Ben   Yes, ⁵ __f ⁶ c__ __rs__.
Monica Can I ⁷ h__v__ ⁸ s__m__ chocolate ice cream too ?
Ben   ⁹ H__r__ you ¹⁰ __r__.
Monica Thanks.

___/10

Your score	**Your total score**
	___/40

☺ 31–40   ☺ 21–30   ☹ 0–20

22

My Picture Dictionary

Stories

1 Look at the pictures. Complete the puzzle.

Discover **5** extra words. Go to page 87.

Talking Tips!

1 Complete the cartoons. Use these sentences.

That's impossible!   Slow down!   Don't panic!
I'm freezing!

Time expressions

2 Read the sentences. Complete the time expressions.

1 Today is 20th August. 6th August was t**wo** w**eeks** a**go** .

2 Today is 20th March. 10th March was t__ __ d__ __ __ a__ __ .

3 It is six o'clock. Two o'clock was f__ __ __ h__ __ __ __ a__ __ .

4 It is October. September was l__ __ __ m__ __ __ __ .

5 It is 2013. 2012 was l__ __ __ y__ __ __ .

3 Imagine it's 31st December. How long ago was…

1 31st October?   *two months ago*
2 21st December?   _____
3 24th December?   _____
4 Christmas Day?   _____
5 31st July?   _____
6 your birthday?   _____

4 Look at the pictures. Write questions. Use *ago* or *last*.

 1 *Where were you five hours ago?*

2 _____?

3 _____?

4 _____?

5 _____?

5 Answer the questions in Exercise 4 for you.

1 _____
2 _____
3 _____
4 _____
5 _____

was / were

6 ⭐⭐ This is the story from Exercise 1. It's mixed up! Number the lines in the correct order.

a Suddenly the woman wasn't there!   ____
b It was a very cold night.   _1_
c There was a tall thin woman in the trees.   ____
d Where was she?   ____
e Andy was scared but Kay wasn't scared.   ____
f Andy and Kay went for a walk.   ____
g Was she a ghost?   _7_

7 ⭐ Circle the correct words.

Yesterday afternoon there ¹ (was)/ were a scary film on TV. There ² **was / were** some ghosts in it. I ³ **was / were** very scared! Mum and Dad ⁴ **wasn't / weren't** there. I ⁵ **was / wasn't** hungry but I didn't eat. There ⁶ **was / wasn't** a pizza in the kitchen but the film ⁷ **was / were** called 'Pizza Panic'. I didn't go in the kitchen!

8 ⭐ Look at the table. Complete the sentences.

	Katie	Ben	Yoda
an hour ago	football match	cinema	school
last week	cinema	football match	football match
ten days ago	school	school	cinema

1 An hour ago Katie **_was_** at a football match.
2 She _____ at the cinema last week.
3 Last week Ben and Yoda _____ .
4 They _____ at the cinema last week.
5 Ben _____ at a football match an hour ago.
6 Katie and Ben _____ at school ten days ago.

9 ⭐⭐ Order the words.

1 last Where you week were
Where were you last week _____ ?
2 ago hour Where you were an
_____ ?
3 Where your were last family summer
_____ ?
4 were weekend your Where friends last
_____ ?

10 ⭐⭐⭐ Answer the questions in Exercise 9 for you.

1 _____
_____
2 _____
_____
3 _____
_____
4 _____

Past simple regular

1 ☆ Match the verbs and the past simple forms.

1 travel	a danced
2 walk	b looked
3 stop	c walked
4 look	d travelled
5 dance	e stopped

Past simple irregular

2 ☆ Match the verbs and the past simple forms.

1 hide	a took
2 be	b ate
3 drink	c hid
4 take	d drank
5 eat	e found
6 find	f was/were

Past simple regular and irregular

3 ☆☆ Complete the sentences. Use verbs in the past simple (affirmative).

1 Yesterday I **_studied_** English for two hours.
2 I _____ to the cinema with my friends at the weekend.
3 My brother _____ a yeti on Monday.
4 We _____ a football match last night.
5 I _____ a noise in the night.
6 I _____ under the bed.

4 ☆☆☆ Tick the sentences in Exercise 3 that are true for you. Correct the sentences that are false for you.

_____
_____
_____
_____
_____

5 ☆ Change these verbs to the affirmative past simple.

1	didn't hear	**_heard_**
2	didn't have	_____
3	didn't like	_____
4	didn't go	_____
5	didn't make	_____
6	didn't watch	_____
7	didn't see	_____
8	weren't	_____
9	wasn't	_____
10	didn't hide	_____

6 ☆☆ Complete the story. Use the verbs in Exercise 5.

Last summer we ¹ **_went_** to Poland on holiday. We ² _____ a scary story about a dragon in Krakow. Is it true?

A long time ago, a dragon lived in a cave near a small town. The people in the town ³ _____ scared. The dragon ⁴ _____ them in the day and at night it ate their sheep and ⁵ _____ in its cave.

One day the girls from the town went to the cave and there they ⁶ _____ the dragon. It ⁷ _____ big teeth and was very scary.

A very clever man heard the story of the dragon. He ⁸ _____ some food for it. It wasn't good food. It was a stir-fry with bad food in it. The dragon ⁹ _____ it. It was hungry and ate it all. Suddenly fire came from its mouth! There ¹⁰ _____ a horrible noise and the dragon disappeared! Today a lot of people go to see the dragon's cave. It's dark and spooky!

7 ⭐⭐ **Read the text again. Answer the questions.**

1 Where did the dragon live?
   It lived in a cave.
2 What did the dragon do at night?
   _____
3 What did the clever man do?
   _____
4 What came out of the dragon's mouth?
   _____
5 What happened to the dragon?
   _____

8 ⭐⭐ **Write negative sentences about the story. Use the words in the table.**

The dragon The clever man The people The girls The sheep	didn't	like make see eat live	good food. the dragon. the bad food. in England. the dragon at night.

1 *The dragon didn't live in England.*
2 _____
   _____
3 _____
   _____
4 _____
   _____
5 _____
   _____
6 _____
   _____

9 ⭐⭐ **True or false? Make the sentences true for you.**

1 Last summer I went to a lake.
   _____
2 At school we read a book about a dragon.
   _____
3 Last week I saw a scary film.
   _____
4 I heard a funny story on Saturday.
   _____

Writing

10 **Answer the questions to make a short story. Use the words in the boxes to help you.**

Where did you go?   (lake   forest   beach)

What did you hear?   (noise   footsteps   singing)

What did you see?   (monster   alien   ghost)

What did you do?   (hide   run   shout)

What happened?   (disappear   fall)

_____
_____
_____
_____
_____
_____
_____
_____
_____
_____

1 Circle the verbs and underline the nouns.

lookmapmakekeylookedboattreasuremade

Past simple questions

2 ☆ Look at Exercise 1. Write:

a the regular past simple verb _____

b the irregular past simple verb _____

3 ☆ Look at the book cover. Match the questions and answers.

1 Did the crabs make a boat?

2 Did they see a crocodile on the beach?

3 Did a pirate follow them?

4 Did the crocodile have a map?

a No, he didn't.

b Yes, they did.

c No, they didn't.

d Yes, he did.

4 ☆ Complete the dialogue. Use these answers.

> We found it in a cave.
> What ring? Oh! I don't know!
> Yes, I went with Jill and Will.
> No, I didn't take it.

Police officer Sit down, Bill. Did you go to the island?

Pirate Bill 1 _____

Police officer Where did you find the treasure?

Pirate Bill 2 _____

Police officer Did you take it?

Pirate Bill 3 _____

Police officer So, where did the parrot get this ring?

Pirate Bill 4 _____

Asking for more information

5 Complete the table. Use the underlined phrases.

1 AJ is <u>Danny's friend</u>.
2 They are <u>on an island</u>.
3 They found <u>a map</u>.
4 The pirates came to the island <u>a long time ago</u>.
5 They went <u>because they were scared</u>.

What?	Why?	Who?	Where?	When?
		Danny's friend		

6 Complete the questions. Write answers from Exercise 5.

1 *Who* is AJ?
AJ is Danny's friend.
2 _____ are they?
They are _____.
3 _____ did they find?
_____
4 _____ did the pirates come?
_____
5 _____ did they go?
_____

7 Complete Bonzo's poem. Use these words.

> see   like   found   thinking

Bonzo's Notes

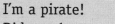

I'm a pirate!
Did you ¹_____?
I ²_____ the map.
Clever me!
Nipper didn't ³_____ it.
Nipper is sad.
What's he ⁴_____?
Horrible crab!

8 Read Bonzo's poem again. Answer the questions.

1 What did Bonzo find?
_____

2 Did he see a pirate?
_____

3 Was Nipper happy?
_____

Nipper's Learning Blog

Remember past simple verbs!

Write new verbs in a notebook.

Put them in sentences.

> find
>
> She found the key in a box.

Reading

1 These two stories are mixed up.
Write them in order.

They sang songs on the boat and took photos.
~~The Robinson family went out for the day.~~
They went on a boat on the lake.
~~Jules was on the beach one day.~~
It was hot and he was bored.
He saw a girl playing with a ball.
It was cold and they didn't swim.
It came from the lake.
He painted his face with strawberry ice cream.
Then he hid behind a rock.
He wanted to play a joke on the girl.
Suddenly they heard a noise.

Story A

1 *The Robinson family went out for the day.*
2 _____
3 _____
4 _____
5 _____
6 _____

Story B

1 *Jules was on the beach one day.*
2 _____
3 _____
4 _____
5 _____
6 _____

2 Match the pictures with the two stories in Exercise 1.

① Story _____

② Story _____

Writing

3 Choose a story from Exercise 1 and write the title. Then imagine and draw the end of the story.

_____

4 Now write the end of the story.

_____
_____
_____
_____
_____
_____

Cities

My Picture Dictionary

Places adjectives

1 Choose five adjectives for each picture. Use these words.

> boring   cheap   clean   dirty   dry   exciting
> expensive   noisy   quiet   wet

① _____
_____
_____
_____

② _____
_____
_____
_____

2 Complete the sentences.

My town is _____ and _____ .
My street is _____ .

1 Complete the adjectives.

1 sm _a_ ll
2 n _ _ _ sy
3 d _ rty
4 _ ld
5 ch _ _ p
6 dr _
7 _ xc _ t _ ng
8 h _ t

a w _ t
b b _ r _ ng
c n _ w
d _ xp _ ns _ v _
e b _ g
f c _ ld
g cl _ _ _ n
h q _ _ _ _ t

2 Match the opposites in Exercise 1.

1 _e_   5 _____
2 _____   6 _____
3 _____   7 _____
4 _____   8 _____

Comparatives and superlatives

3 ⭐ Write the words in the correct column.

the driest   ~~nicer~~   noisier   the coolest   cheap
the noisiest   older   cheaper

adjective	comparative	superlative
nice	¹ _nicer_	the nicest
² _____	³ _____	the cheapest
cool	cooler	⁴ _____
old	⁵ _____	the oldest
dry	drier	⁶ _____
noisy	⁷ _____	⁸ _____
_____	_____	_____
_____	_____	_____
_____	_____	_____

4 ⭐⭐ Complete the text. Use words from Exercise 3.

COVENT GARDEN

The ¹ _coolest_ place to go in London is Covent Garden. A long time ago it was a fruit market but it's ² **n**_____ now! There are cafés, shops and a big market with souvenirs. The market is ³ **c**_____ than the shops, but it's ⁴ **n**_____ too. I love it!
London is not the ⁵ **d**_____ city in the world – it rains a lot. But every day there are entertainers in the street, acrobats and singers and dancers. Drury Lane is the ⁶ **o**_____ theatre in Covent Garden, but the tickets aren't ⁷ **c**_____ .

5 ⭐⭐ Look at the table in Exercise 3. Add the adjectives *big*, *hot* and *quiet* and their comparative and superlative forms.

Talking Tips!

6 Match the sentences with the people.

1 | I feel terrible!

2 | What an amazing view!

3 | Slow down!

Ⓐ   Ⓑ   Ⓒ

7 ⭐ Look at the picture in Exercise 6. Write A, B or C.

1 She's the tallest.   *C*
2 She's the oldest.   _____
3 She's the smallest.   _____
4 She's the noisiest.   _____
5 She's the happiest.   _____

8 ⭐ Complete the sentences.

1 A is taller than ___*B*___ .
2 B is _____ than A.
3 A is the noisiest and the _____ .
4 C is happier than _____ and _____ .
5 B is the _____ .
6 A is older _____ and _____ .

Writing

9 Complete the poster for a new restaurant in Covent Garden. Give your restaurant a name. Use these words and superlatives.

> kitchens / clean   restaurant / cool
> food / nice   cakes / cheap
> drinks / big   dining room / new

Our kitchens are the cleanest!

Places in town

1 Find the places in town.

1	o	r	r	b	a	h	u			_harbour_
2	w	o	r	t	e					_____
3	b	g	d	r	i	e				_____
4	p	o	i	a	r	r	t			_____
5	e	e	t	t	a	h	r			_____
6	s	m	e	m	u	u				_____
7	e	t	u	r	a	s	n	t	r a	_____
8	t	r	o	p	s	s				
	d	i	m	u	a	t	s			_____ _____
9	n	t	w	o	q u	e	s	a r		_____ _____
10	g	s	p	h	p	o	n	i		
	r	e	e	n	t	c				_____ _____

Comparatives and superlatives

2 ☆ Match the syllables to make words.

ful	ring	~~ex~~	bo	~~ting~~	beau

mous	ti	fa	~~ci~~

1 _ex_ + _ci_ + _ting_ = _exciting_
2 ____ + ____ + ____ = _____
3 ____ + ____ = _____
4 ____ + ____ = _____

3 ☆ Complete the text. Use *good*, *better*, *the best*, *bad* or *the worst*.

I like my town, it's a ¹ _**good**_ (good) place to live. Last summer was ² _____ (bad) summer in history. It rained every day! We weren't bored. We've got ³ _____ (good) sports stadium in the country. It's ⁴ _____ (good) than an Olympic stadium. ⁵ _____ (bad) thing is that it is expensive. A family ticket is cheaper, only £3. That isn't too ⁶ _____ (bad).

4 ☆☆ Write sentences. Use comparative forms of the words in brackets.

1 bus / taxi (expensive)
   **The taxi is more expensive than the bus.**

2 a helicopter ride / a museum (exciting)
   _____

3 surfing / swimming (dangerous)
   _____

4 The theatre / town square (interesting)
   _____

5 Sydney, Australia / Sydney, Canada (famous)
   _____

Reading

5 Look, read and answer the questions.

1 How many bridges can you see? _____
2 Is Tower Bridge in picture A or B? _____
3 Is Tower Bridge in London or San Francisco? _____
4 Which bridge did Rhonda want? _____

The Tale of Two Bridges

Rhonda Rich Wow, is that London Bridge? It's the most famous bridge in the world!

Bad Ed Well, it's a bridge and it's in London. It's very old. It's older than the Golden Gate Bridge in San Francisco.

Rhonda Rich I want to buy it!

Bad Ed OK, but it's very expensive!

They are building the bridge. Rhonda Rich is watching. She calls Bad Ed.

Rhonda Rich Hey, that isn't London Bridge! It's smaller and it isn't beautiful!

Bad Ed Sorry, Rhonda, that is London Bridge. Oh dear! Was it Tower Bridge you wanted?

6 Read the dialogues again. True or false?

1 London Bridge is newer than Golden Gate Bridge. *false*
2 Tower Bridge is the oldest bridge in San Francisco. _____
3 Rhonda Rich thinks Tower Bridge is more beautiful than London Bridge. _____
4 Rhonda Rich wants to buy the smallest bridge in London. _____
5 The Golden Gate Bridge is the oldest bridge in the world. _____
6 There are famous bridges in London and San Francisco. _____

7 Order the words. Write the question.

A | Is | Tower | the | in | Bridge | famous | bridge | London | most |

_____?

B Yes, it is!

8 Complete the dialogue between Rhonda Rich's friends. Use comparative and superlative forms of the words in brackets.

A Rhonda Rich is going to London again. It's
¹ _____ (exciting) place in the world!

B Really? I like New York better. It's
² _____ (beautiful) London.

A Ah, but New York is ³ _____ (dangerous) London.

B Yes, but London is so expensive. It's
⁴ _____
(expensive) city in the world. Rhonda loves it!

too and enough

1 ⭐ Match the sentences with a similar meaning.

1 It's too small!   a It isn't cold enough.
2 It's too expensive!   b It isn't big enough.
3 It's too boring!   c It isn't quiet enough.
4 It's too noisy!   d It isn't cheap enough.
5 It's too hot!   e It isn't exciting enough.

2 ⭐⭐ Look and write two sentences for each T-shirt. Use *too* and *enough* and a suitable adjective.

1 *It's too small. It isn't big enough.*
2 _____
3 _____
4 _____
5 _____

3 Circle three adjectives.

4 ⭐⭐ Write three sentences about the bridge on the island. Use the adjectives from Exercise 3 and *too* or *enough*.

1 It isn't _____ enough.
2 _____
3 _____

5 Separate the words of Bonzo's poem.

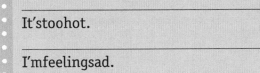

Bonzo's Notes

Thedaywasbadatfirst.
The day was bad at first.
NowIthinkit'sworse.
_____

It'stoohot.
_____

I'mfeelingsad.
_____

Poorme!It'stoobad!
_____

Thetreewasveryhigh.
_____

AndnowIwanttocry.
_____

Itisn'tsafe.
_____

I'mfeelingbad.
_____

Ohno!Iwantmydad!
_____

6 Find the opposites of these words in Bonzo's Notes.

1 good   *bad*
2 dangerous   _____
3 yes   _____
4 happy   _____
5 better   _____

Making suggestions

7 Order the words.

1 a walk about What for going
What about going for a walk?

2 map How looking the at about
_____ ?

3 a take Let's drink
_____

4 food some about How too
_____ ?

5 about picnic What helping the with
_____ ?

6 river the What to going about
_____ ?

8 Make suggestions for Bonzo. Use the phrases in the table to make sentences.

How about What about Why don't you	having a swim? drink some water? be quiet? going for a walk in the forest?

1 *Why don't you drink some water?*
2 _____ ?
3 _____ ?
4 _____ ?

9 Make four suggestions about what to do on a desert island. Use *How / What about*, *Let's* or *Why don't you* and some of these phrases.

> make a hut   catch fish   look for coconuts
> build a boat   make a fire   cook crabs
> sing songs   write in the sand   play games

1 _____
2 _____
3 _____
4 _____

Nipper's Learning Blog

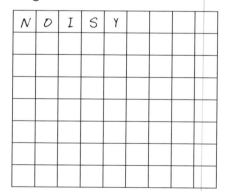

Remember adjectives!

1 Choose 6–8 adjectives.
2 Write a letter in each square. The words can go across or down the puzzle.
3 Use a pencil and use capital letters.
4 Complete the puzzle with vowels. Then give it to a friend!

N	O	I	S	Y				

Vocabulary

1 Write the opposites.

1 dry _____
2 expensive _____
3 clean _____
4 boring _____
5 quiet _____

2 Circle the correct words.

1 It's the longest **tower / bridge** in the country.
2 How about playing football in the **sports stadium / theatre**?
3 Let's have lunch in a **restaurant / airport**!
4 Sydney has a very famous **museum / harbour**.
5 The **shopping centre / town square** in the village is hundreds of years old.
6 There's a new shop in the **shopping centre / tower**.

___/11

Grammar

3 Complete the table. Use these words.

the best   bad   the worst   better

adjective	comparative	superlative
good	1 _____	2 _____
3 _____	worse	4 _____

4 Bert is bad but Brenda is worse. Complete the sentences. Use comparatives.
Terrible Twins!

1 Bert's room is dirty but Brenda's is _____!
2 His music is noisy but hers is _____!
3 His pet is dangerous but hers is _____!
4 His shoes are wet but hers are _____!
5 His homework is bad but _____!
6 At school, Bert is famous but _____!

5 Complete Beth's paragraphs. Use adjectives, comparatives or superlatives.

London is [1] _____ (interesting) city in the world! It isn't a [2] _____ (friendly) city but it is [3] _____ (exciting) city I know.

My cousin, Ben is [4] _____ (old) than me. His school in London is [5] _____ (big) than my school. The food is [6] _____ (good) than in my school too. The sausages are [7] _____ (good) in the world!

6 Complete the sentences. Use opposites.

Beth wants to climb Mount Kilimanjaro.

Beth's mum says:
It's too dangerous!
[2] _____
You're too young!
It's too hot!
[5] _____
It's too big!

Beth's dad says:
[1] It isn't _____ enough.
It isn't cheap enough.
[3] _____
[4] _____
It isn't easy enough.
[6] _____

___/23

Functions

7 Make suggestions. Use the words in brackets.

1 How about _____? (tennis)
2 Let's _____. (TV)
3 What about _____? (bike ride)
4 What _____? (museum)
5 Let's _____. (shopping)
6 How _____? (swim)

___/6

Your score	Your total score
	___/40

☺ 31–40   ☺ 21–30   ☹ 0–20

5 Explore!

My Picture Dictionary

The natural world

1 Circle the places you can find in your country.

jungle   canyon   ~~glacier~~   cave   volcano   river   desert   ocean

glacier

2 Label the photos with the words in Exercise 1.

_____

_____

_____

_____

_____

_____

_____

3 Find the answer.

What is the name of the biggest ocean in the world?

HTE   IAFCPCI   CONAE

The _____ _____

my words

Do you know more words that describe the natural world? Write them here.

_____
_____
_____
_____

5ᵃ Around The World

Talking Tips!

1 Complete the dialogue. Use these words.

> ~~freezing~~   Don't panic   amazing view
> Never mind   feel terrible

Jack Oh Jill, I'm ¹ _**freezing**_!
Jill What an ² _____ _____!
Jack Oh no!
      I ³ _____ _____!
Jill ⁴ N _____ _____ ⁵ D _____
      _____!

Numbers 100–1,000,000

2 Order the numbers. Write the smallest number first.

> six thousand five hundred and fifty-five
> nine hundred and eighty
> one million
> thirty thousand five hundred
> ~~one hundred~~
> eight hundred and twenty thousand

1 _**one hundred**_ _____
2 _____
3 _____
4 _____
5 _____
6 _____

3 Look and write the numbers.

On Mount Kilimanjaro the climber stopped at …
1 one thousand four hundred metres.
     _**1,400**_
2 four thousand seven hundred and three metres.
     _____
3 two thousand eight hundred metres.
     _____
4 three thousand seven hundred and twenty metres. _____
5 The mountain is _____
     metres high. It's the highest mountain in Africa!

4 Read the article. Circle the numbers in the text. Write them as words.

The islands of Hawaii are in the Pacific Ocean. They are ⟨3,200⟩ kilometres from the coast of the United States. There are 2,400 kilometres of islands! There are hundreds of them.

The islands are volcanoes and they are millions of years old. Some are very small, some are bigger and have rivers and lakes. The biggest is called Big Island, and has a famous National Park. There is a very big cave in the park called Kazumuru cave. It is 61,420 metres long and 1,102 metres deep. It is the deepest cave in the USA and you can walk in there for 8 hours.

Hawaii is famous for its beaches and flowers. There is a desert in Kau. Half of the mountain is very dry and half is wet. The rainforest is a type of jungle.
There is never a bad time to visit Hawaii. It is always beautiful!

1 *three thousand two hundred* kilometres
2 _____ kilometres
3 _____ metres
4 _____ metres
5 _____ hours

Questions with *how*

5 ☆☆ Order the words.

1 | walk in | can you | the cave | How long |
   How long can you walk in the cave?
2 | are the | How far | US coast | from the | islands |

   _____?
3 | of islands | How many | are there | kilometres |

   _____?
4 | the cave | How deep | is |

   _____?
5 | is | the cave | How long |

   _____?

6 Read the text in Exercise 4 again. Answer the questions in Exercise 5.

1 *You can walk in the cave for eight hours.*
2 _____
3 _____
4 _____
5 _____

Writing

7 Look at the table and write the questions and answers. Use these adjectives.

⟨ deep   long   wide   high ⟩

name	size
Grand Canyon	16 km wide
Amazon River	6,400 km long
Lake Baikal	1,620 m deep
Mount Everest	8,850 m high

1 How wide is the widest canyon?
   It's 16 km wide.
2 How long _____?
3 _____?
   _____?
4 _____?
   _____?

8 Complete the text with facts about a famous place in your country.

In _____ there is a _____.
It's called _____.
It's _____ long / high / deep.

going to

1 ⭐⭐ Write affirmative and negative sentences. Use one word or phrase from each cloud.

He She It They We

visit see watch study be

going to

today tomorrow next week on Wednesday

a museum rainy Grandmother history a match

is isn't are aren't

affirmative
1 *He is going to watch a match tomorrow.*
2 _____
3 _____
4 _____
negative
5 *They aren't going to visit a museum today.*
6 _____
7 _____
8 _____

2 ⭐⭐ Rewrite the sentences. Use *going to* and the words in brackets.

1 I'm wearing boots.   (tomorrow)
   I'm going to wear boots tomorrow.
2 We're eating in a restaurant.   (this evening)
   _____
3 My teacher's painting the school.   (next week)
   _____
4 We don't have any homework.   (tomorrow)
   _____
5 I'm not climbing a mountain.   (next year)
   _____

3 ⭐⭐⭐ Are the sentences in Exercise 2 true for you? Correct the false sentences.

1 *false   I'm not going to wear boots tomorrow.*
2 _____
3 _____
4 _____
5 _____

4 ⭐⭐ Look at Ben's plans for the weekend. Complete the questions and answers.

This weekend:
buy sun cream
look for camera
clean hiking boots
paint bike
call Monica
do homework

1
A Is Ben **going to** buy sunglasses?
B No, he isn't. He's **going to buy sun cream**.
2
A Is he _____ his camera?
B Yes, he is.
3
A Is he _____ clean his bike?
B No _____ . He's _____ .
4
A Is he _____ do his _____?
B Yes, he is.
5
A Is he _____ call Ravi?
B No _____ . He's _____ .

5 ⭐⭐⭐ Write about your plans for this weekend.

1 I'm going to _____
2 _____
3 I'm not going to _____
4 _____

Reading

6 The story is mixed up! Number the paragraphs in the correct order.

You Can Do It!

A ☐
Monty showed his homework to his teacher. 'This is impossible, Monty. Do your homework again!' Monty didn't repeat his homework. 'I'm going to follow my dream!' Today, Monty lives in his beautiful house with horses in the garden.

B ☐
Monty was a young boy in a new school. His family didn't have a lot of money.
One day his teacher said 'For homework you are going to write a story. The story is going to be about YOU! It is going to be about your future.'

C ☐
Monty was excited. He wrote 'I'm going to buy a field! Then I'm going to build a house. It isn't going to be a small house. It's going to have lots of rooms and a big garden with a pool. I'm going to have horses in the garden too.'

7 Who said it? Write M (Monty) or T (his teacher).

1 I'm going to have horses in the garden.   _M_
2 You are going to write a story.   _____
3 I'm going to buy a field!   _____
4 It isn't going to be a small house.   _____
5 It is going to be about your future.   _____
6 I'm going to follow my dream!   _____

8 Look at the plans for a swimming pool. Write the questions and answers. Use the words in brackets.

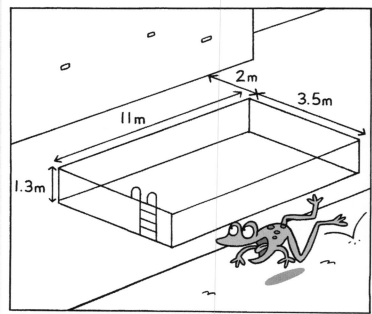

1 (deep)
How deep is it going to be?
It's going to be 1.3 m deep.

2 (long)
_____
_____

3 (wide)
_____
_____

4 (far from the house)
_____
_____ away from the house.

5c Adventure Island

Prepositions of movement

1 Find six prepositions of movement in the word square.

A	W	A	Y	F	R	O	M
Q	R	E	R	G	K	V	N
H	B	O	U	N	D	E	R
J	Y	I	U	P	L	R	V
V	D	L	X	N	M	D	K
T	O	W	A	R	D	S	T
Z	T	H	R	O	U	G	H

2 Label the pictures with prepositions of movement.

1 _**away from**_

2 _____

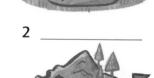

3 _____

4 _____

5 _____

6 _____

3 Look at the map. Complete the sentences.

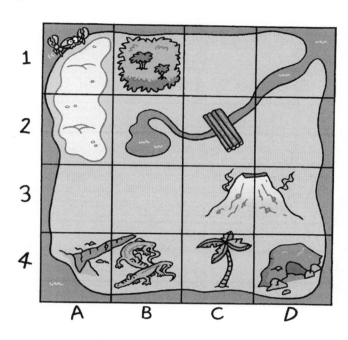

1 There's a desert in A1 and **A2**.
2 In B1 there is a _____ .
3 A river goes from D1, _____ C2 into a lake in B2.
4 There is a bridge over the _____ in C2.
5 In C3 and _____ there is a volcano.
6 C4 has got a big tree. There is a big cave behind it in _____ .

Following directions

4 Read and follow Bad Crab's route on the map in Exercise 3. Where is he now?

Bad Crab is on the island.
He is going to find the treasure.
He walks away from the desert and then runs through the jungle.
He goes towards the river and over the bridge.
Then Bad Crab walks around the volcano and under the big palm tree.
Then he goes into the _____ .

44

5 Write the directions.

1 Bad Crab is on the bridge. How does he get to the palm tree?
Go across the bridge.
Go around the volcano.

2 Bad Crab is on the bridge. How does he get to the canyon?

_____

_____

3 Bad Crab is in the cave. How does he get to the desert?

_____

_____

_____

_____

6 Complete Bonzo's poem with these words.

me   bad   ~~day~~   tree   crab   say   away

Bonzo's Notes

What a walk!
What a [1] *day*!
Who is this girl?
Who can [2] _____?

I'm going to cry.
I'm feeling [3] _____
My life's in the hands
Of a horrible [4] _____!

I can't walk [5] _____,
Or hide in a [6] _____
I don't like this girl!
It's the end for [7] _____!

7 Answer the questions about the poem in Exercise 6.

1 Who does Bonzo see on the walk?

_____

_____

2 Can he walk away?

_____

3 Can he hide?

_____

_____

4 Does he like the girl?

_____

_____

Nipper's Learning Blog

Talking about the future

Every day write one thing that you are going to do tomorrow.

Tomorrow I'm going to clean my room.

5d Different Lives

Reading

1 Read Ben's postcard. Answer the questions.

Hi Katie!

We are having a fantastic holiday in the US.

Next week we are going to travel along Route 66. Route 66 is a very long road that goes from Chicago across the USA to Santa Monica in California. We are going to see some wonderful sights. What an adventure!

The Mother Road or Route 66, is more than 3,864 kilometres long and goes through eight states. We will go over mountains and across rivers. We are not going to stay long in each place but I'm going to take lots of photos. I want to remember every minute!

See you soon.

Ben

1 What is Route 66?

_____

2 What is another name for Route 66?

_____

3 What will Ben see along the way?

_____

4 What is he going to do to help him remember the trip?

_____

2 Look at Ben's postcard. Find and circle:

Three numbers
Four prepositions of movement
Two cities
Two natural world words.

Writing

3 Write the names of three natural sights in your country.

1 _____
2 _____
3 _____

4 Choose one place in your country to go to. Complete the paragraph for a guidebook.

Explore _____ !

Your trip is going to start in _____ .
You are going to see _____ .
_____ is very high / old / famous / beautiful.
Then you are going to see _____ .
It's _____ .

My Picture Dictionary

Space

1 Label the picture. Use these words

telescope   space suit   ~~Earth~~   alien   space station   star
Moon   astronaut   spaceship

① Earth

②

③

④

⑤

⑥

⑦

⑧

⑨

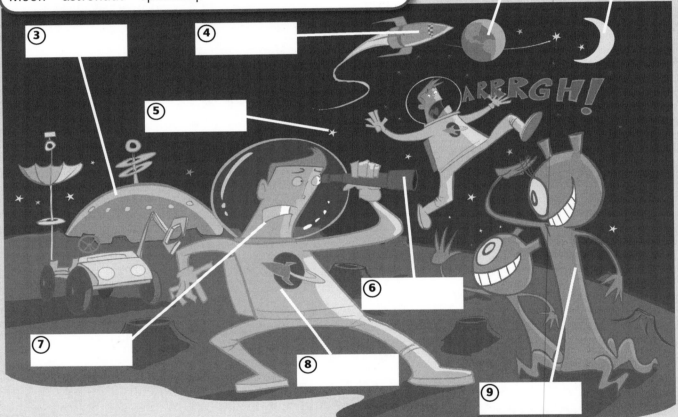

2 Circle the words you can make from this word.

astronaut

earth   sun   moon   star

3 Complete the sentence with words from Exercise 1.

An ¹ _____ wearing a ² _____
is going to the Moon in a ³ _____!

my words

Do you know more space words?
Write them here.

_____
_____
_____

Chores

1 Find eight of these words in the word square. Circle the words you find.

> clean   bed   dishes   (clothes)   space
> suit   make   do   wash   shoes   wear

C	A	B	J	L	P
L	L	U	E	V	I
O	D	E	M	D	X
T	F	H	A	M	S
H	R	Y	K	N	H
E	Z	K	E	D	O
S	W	A	S	H	E
D	I	S	H	E	S

2 Complete the phrases with words from Exercise 1.

1 make the _____
2 _____ the shoes
3 wash the _____
4 _____ the dishes

have to

3 ⭐⭐ Which chores do you have to do? Write sentences. Use these words.

> cook the food
> tidy the house
> empty the bin
> wash the car
> make the bed
> walk the dog

> every day
> once a week
> once a month
> never

1 *I have to walk the dog every day.*
2 _____
3 _____
4 _____
5 _____

4 ⭐ Look at the table. Read and write the names.

	empty bin	make bed	clean shoes	do dishes
Ben	0000	000	00	00
Monica	0	0000	0000	000
Ravi	0000	0	00	0
Katie	00	0000	0	0

> 0000 = every day   000 = at the weekend
> 00 = once a week   0 = never

1
I make my bed every day but I never have to clean my shoes or do the dishes.
I have to empty the bin every Saturday.

_____

2
On Sunday nights I have to clean my shoes and once a week I have to do the dishes. I only have to make my bed at the weekend. In the week my mum usually does it! I have to empty the bin after school every day.

_____

3
I make my bed every day and I have to clean my shoes every day too. I don't have to empty the bin and I only do the dishes at the weekend.

_____

5 ⭐⭐ Look at the table again. Write sentences about Ravi's chores. Use *He has to* or *He doesn't have to*.

1 *He has to empty the bin every day.*
2 _____
3 _____
4 _____

Discover **5** extra words. Go to page 87.

adventure Magazine

March 2010

Read about Lloyd Godson's new mission!
He isn't an astronaut, he's an *aqua*naut!
What's that?
Well, an astronaut visits space and does experiments.
Lloyd does experiments too but he does them under water.

6 ⭐⭐ Read the article. Order the words to make questions.

1 long he have stay to does How there

  How long does he have to stay there?

2 days he food to Does have take for thirteen

  _____
  _____?

3 exercise he have to Does do

  _____
  _____?

4 we emails Can send him

  _____
  _____?

5 we too see Can him

  _____
  _____?

6 water Does under Lloyd living like

  _____
  _____?

7 ⭐⭐ Match the answers with the questions in Exercise 6.

___6___ **a** Yes. It was always his dream and it came true!

_____ **b** Yes. He has to take a computer and give us a report every day.

_____ **c** Yes, he does. Exercise is very important.

_____ **d** He has to stay thirteen days for his experiments.

_____ **e** No, he doesn't. His friends bring him food.

_____ **f** Yes, we can. He's got a webcam on the computer.

8 ⭐ Complete the sentence. Use these words.

(have dream have dream)

You _____ to _____ a _____ for the _____ to come true!

Talking Tips!

1 Complete the dialogue. Use these sentences.

> Don't panic! Perfect! I doubt it!

A Is that our spaceship?
B ¹ _____ Ours is bigger.
A Can I take my telescope?
B It's very heavy.
A ² _____ I can carry it.
B ³ _____

will future

2 ☆ Circle the odd one out.

1 in 2033 in the future (now) next week
2 tomorrow yesterday next spring next year
3 at the moment next Christmas later today
  in 2013
4 next winter in 2020 in 1974 next Saturday

3 ☆☆ Change these sentences from the past simple to the future. Use *will* or *won't*.

1 Ravi didn't do any homework.
  Ravi won't do any homework.
2 He bought a robot.
  _____
3 They didn't go to the Moon.
  _____
4 They ate space food.
  _____
5 They wore helmets.
  _____
6 They didn't meet aliens.
  _____

4 ☆ Answer the questions using information from Exercise 3. Use these words.

Yes	he	will
No	they	won't

1 Will Ravi do any homework?
  No, he won't.
2 Will he buy a robot?
  _____
3 Will they go to the Moon?
  _____
4 Will they eat space food?
  _____
5 Will he buy a helmet?
  _____
6 Will they meet aliens?
  _____

5 ⭐⭐ Read about Monica's future. Write questions.

My future!

In the future I'll go to California with my friends.

We'll stay in a big hotel and a very important film maker will see us. He'll ask us to work on his new film. We'll go to Hollywood and meet all the stars. We won't be famous at first but after the film we'll be in all the magazines and newspapers.

The film will win an Oscar and I'll wear a long dress. My parents will cry!
I'll be a star!

1 Where / Monica / go
   Where will Monica go?
2 Who / Monica / go / with
   _____
   _____ ?
3 Where / they / stay
   _____
   _____ ?
4 Who / see / them
   _____
   _____ ?
5 Who / they / meet
   _____
   _____ ?
6 What / film / win
   _____
   _____ ?
7 Who / be / star
   _____
   _____ ?

6 ⭐⭐ Read the text in Exercise 5 again. Answer the questions you wrote.

1 *She'll go to California.*
2 _____
3 _____
4 _____
5 _____
6 _____
7 _____

Writing

7 Write about your future. Answer these questions. Use your imagination.

Where will you go?
Who will you go with?
Who will you meet?
Where will you live?
What will you do?

_____
_____
_____
_____
_____

Possessives

1 ⭐ Complete the table.

This is my planet.	It's ¹ _mine_ !
This is ² _____ planet.	It's yours!
This is his planet.	It's ³ _____ !
This is ⁴ _____ planet.	It's hers!
This is its planet.	It's ⁵ _____ !
This is ⁶ _____ planet.	It's ours!
This is their planet.	It's ⁷ _____ !

2 ⭐⭐ Find the names. Complete the sentences.

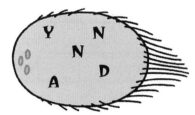

1 It's _Danny's_ coconut. It's _his_ .

2 It's _____ coconut. It's _____ .

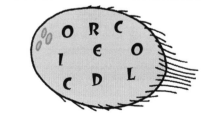

3 It's the _____ coconut. It's _____ .

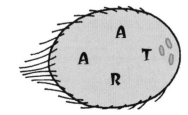

4 It's _____ coconut. It's _____ .

Guessing

3 Order the words.

1 back come think she'll I
   **I think she'll come back.**

2 treasure Maybe find some they'll
   _____

3 I'll have party a probably
   _____

4 you'll think I make friends
   _____

5 probably a He'll tree house make
   _____

4 Look at the spidergram. What will Tara do with the treasure? Write sentences.

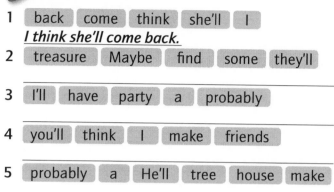

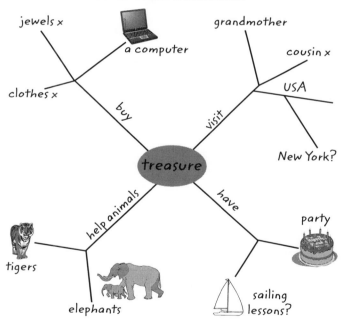

1 _I think she'll visit her grandmother._
2 _She won't visit her cousin._
3 _Maybe she'll visit New York._
4 _____
5 _____
6 _____
7 _____
8 _____

5 Complete Bonzo's poem. Use these words.

| do | alone | OK | home | me | today | ~~true~~ |

Bonzo's Notes

Do wishes come ¹ *true* ?
Mine do for ² _____ .
And yours do for you.
Or maybe they don't.
But I think they ³ _____ .

Tara's ⁴ _____ .
We'll help her ⁵ _____ .
Then we'll go ⁶ _____
And leave her. ⁷ _____ ?

6 What do you think? Tick the table and write sentences. Use *I think*, *maybe* or *probably*.

	maybe	yes	no
1 Will Bonzo's wishes come true?	✓		
2 Will Bonzo help Tara?			
3 Will Bonzo go home soon?			
4 Will your wishes come true?			

1 *Maybe Bonzo's wishes will come true.*
2 _____
   _____
3 _____
   _____
4 _____
   _____

Nipper's Learning Blog

Spidergrams help us to remember!

Draw a spidergram about your next birthday party.

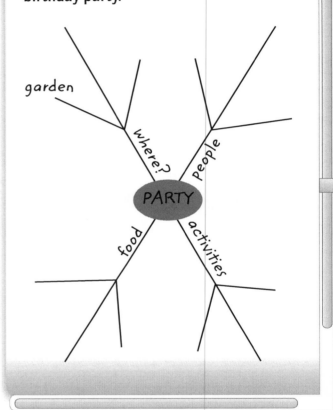

7 Complete the sentences about your party.

1 The party will be in the _____
   _____ .

2 I'll probably invite _____
   _____ .

3 Maybe we'll eat _____
   _____ .

4 I don't think we'll _____
   _____ .

Vocabulary

1 Find the space words.

1 t a i s e p s u c
2 r t a s
3 e o s l c e p t e
4 n a l e p t
5 e a c h p i s p s
6 h r t a E
7 n l e i a
8 o M o n
9 r n u t o t a s a

2 Match the words.

1 wash   the bin
2 empty   the house
3 cook   the bed
4 tidy   clothes
5 make   food

___/14

Grammar

3 Circle the correct words.

1 They're Ravi's shoes. They're **his** / **ours**.
2 It's Ben and Monica's party. It's **hers** / **theirs**.
3 It's my computer. It's **yours** / **mine**.
4 They're Monica's jewels. They're **yours** / **hers**.
5 It's your treasure. It's **yours** / **ours**.
6 They're our friends. They're **ours** / **his**.

4 Write sentences about what Kelly has to or doesn't have to do in space.

1 do the dishes ✗

_____

2 do exercise ✔

_____

3 wear a space suit ✔

_____

4 walk the dog ✗

_____

5 Complete the story about Ben. Use *will* or *won't* and these verbs in the future tense.

come   meet   wear   go

In space, Ben [1] _____ _____ a space suit. He [2] _____ _____ aliens on Saturn. Then he [3] _____ _____ to Venus. He [4] _____ _____ back to Earth in the evening.

6 Order the words.

1 Will on Venus aliens meet Ben
_____?

2 wear Will a he space suit
_____?

3 Earth come to back he Will
_____?

4 he Will go Mars to
_____?

7 Write answers to the questions in Exercise 6. Use *Yes, he will* or *No, he won't*.

1 _____   2 _____
3 _____   4 _____

___/22

Functions

8 Read and write sentences in the future tense. Use the words in brackets.

1 He'll work under water. (probably / be / famous)

_____

2 She'll wear a space suit. (maybe / go / Venus)

_____

3 They'll visit Mars. (I think / go / spaceship)

_____

4 I'll look on the Moon. (I / not see / aliens)

_____

___/4

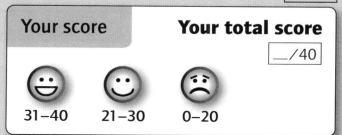

Your score   **Your total score**

___/40

31–40   21–30   0–20

7 Music

My Picture Dictionary

Music and instruments

1 Complete the names of the instruments.

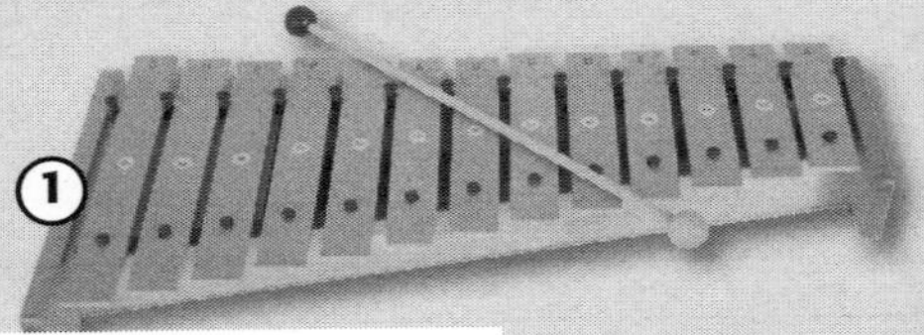

s __ x __ ph __ n __ ②

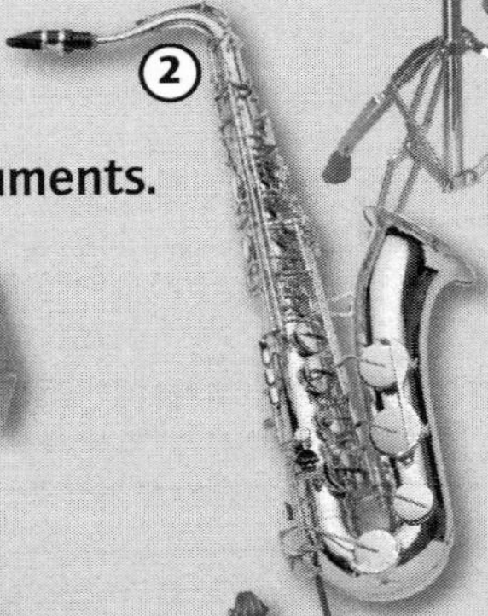

dr __ ms ③

x __ l __ ph __ n __ ①

k __ yb __ __ rd ④

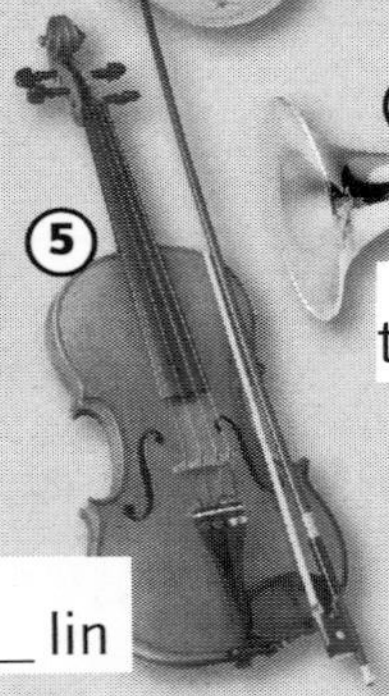

v __ __ lin ⑤

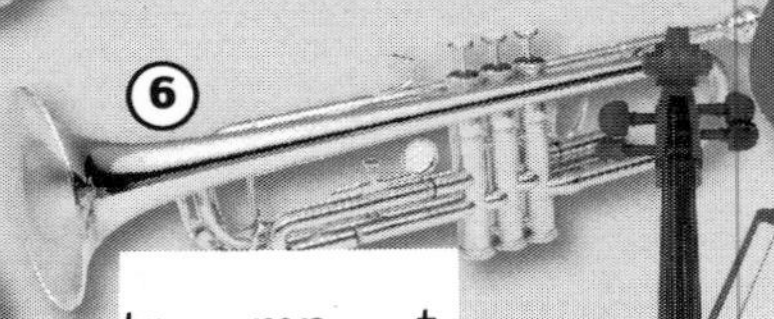

tr __ mp __ t ⑥

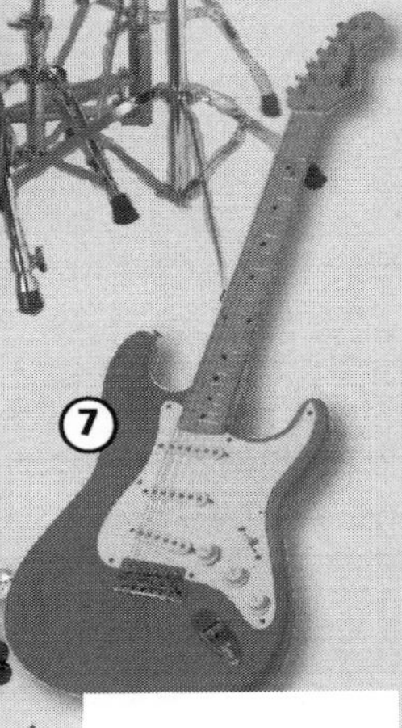

__ l __ ctr __ __
g __ __ tar ⑦

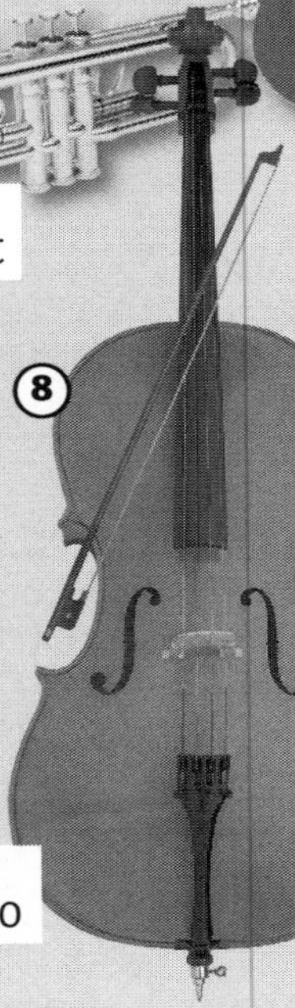

c __ llo ⑧

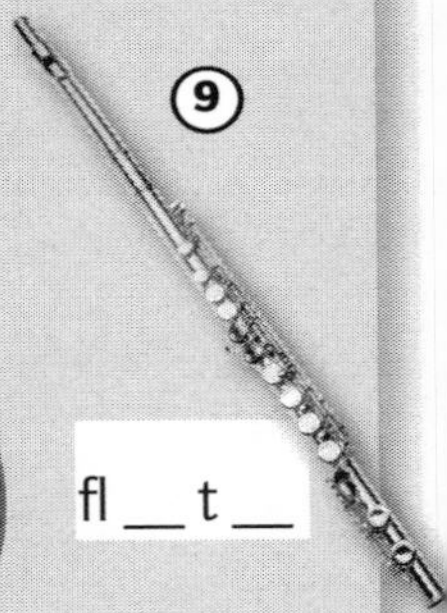

fl __ t __ ⑨

2 What music do they like? Follow the lines and write.
Use these words.

Latin   jazz   folk   pop   classical

Monica
_____

Ravi
_____

Katie
_____

Ben
_____

Yoda
_____

3 Find the type of music Yoda doesn't like.

e v y a h   l e t a m

Yoda doesn't like _____ music.

my words

Do you know more instruments
or music words? Write them
here.

_____
_____
_____
_____

7ᵃ New Stars

Talking Tips!

1 This dialogue is mixed up! Write it in the correct order.

Monica <u>That's impossible!</u> He's really famous.

Ben <u>Calm down</u>, Monica! I haven't started lessons and you haven't practised any songs!

Monica <u>Are you sure?</u> Wow! Get your guitar!

Ben <u>Check this out!</u> Jack Johnson's coming to *New Stars*!

Ben I know, but he's looking for young singers and guitar players.

Ben ¹ ***Check this out! Jack Johnson's coming to*** New Stars*!*

Monica ² _____

Ben ³ _____

Monica ⁴ _____

Ben ⁵ _____

2 Label the pictures. Use the underlined phrases from Exercise 1.

① _____

② _____

③ _____

④ _____

Present perfect

3 ⭐⭐ Complete the table. Circle the regular past participles.

present	past	past participle
play	¹ *played*	played
win	won	² _____
have	³ _____	had
⁴ _____	gave	⁵ _____
write	⁶ _____	written
make	made	⁷ _____
⁸ _____	listened	⁹ _____
¹⁰ _____	heard	heard
¹¹ _____	¹² _____	gone / been

4 ⭐ Circle the correct words.

Monica Look, Dad has ¹ **gave** / **given** me his old keyboard!

Mum When did he ² **gave** / **give** it to you?

Monica This morning. We ³ **go** / **went** down to the garage.

Mum Have you ⁴ **clean** / **cleaned** the bikes this morning?

Dad No, but I've ⁵ **tidy** / **tidied** the garage.

Mum Yes, and you've ⁶ **gave** / **given** your keyboard to Monica.

Dad That's right! We ⁷ **play** / **played** some of my old songs.

5 ⭐⭐ What has Monica's dad done today? Complete the sentences.

1 He's ***given*** his keyboard to Monica.

2 _____ some songs.

3 _____ the garage.

4 But he hasn't _____ .

Discover ⑤ extra words. Go to page 87.

6 ⭐⭐ Read the dialogue. True or false? Correct the false sentences.

Katie Look! There's Ravi, back from the festival! Hi, Ravi!

Monica What festival?

Ravi We've been to the Pop-in-the-Park festival.

Monica Wow! I've heard about it, but I haven't been.

Ravi We've had a wonderful time! We've seen some amazing bands and met some famous people too.

Katie Who?

Ravi The Police, Manu Chau, Coldplay.

Katie I love Coldplay. Mum's given me a CD of their music. Wait a minute! It's here in my bag.

Monica Is it a birthday present?

Katie No. It isn't my birthday but I've passed all my music exams and Mum is really happy.

Ravi Hey! That's great! Let's celebrate!

1 Monica and Katie have been to a pop festival.
   __false   Monica and Katie haven't been to__
   __a pop festival.__

2 Ravi hasn't been to a pop festival.
   _____

3 Katie hasn't passed her music exams.
   _____

4 Katie's mum has given her a Coldplay CD.
   _____

5 Monica and Katie have met some famous people.
   _____

6 Katie's seen some amazing drum kits.
   _____

7 ⭐⭐ Complete Ben's email. Use the past participles of these verbs.

> play   tidy   give   write   make   practise   ~~listen~~   meet   be

Hi Ravi,

I've got the new Coldplay album at last. It's really good and I've ¹ ***listened*** to it about five times! My sister's ² _____ to the Pop-in-the-Park festival too. She's in New York at the moment but she hasn't ³ _____ me an email yet. Lucky her! I'm sure she's ⁴ _____ some famous people. She's probably ⁵ _____ friends with Tom Cruise.

I haven't ⁶ _____ the guitar this week but I've ⁷ _____ my uncle's saxophone. He's ⁸ _____ me some jazz CDs.

We're going out in a minute and I haven't ⁹ _____ my room, so more later!

Ben

Writing

8 ⭐⭐ Look at Nervous Nigel's list of things to do. Write sentences. Use the present perfect.

practise the guitar
tidy my bedroom
watch Top Pops Today ✓
finish my homework
phone granddad ✓
go to the music shop ✓

1 *__He hasn't practised the guitar.__*
2 _____
3 _____
4 _____
5 _____
6 _____

9 ⭐⭐⭐ Write sentences about you. Use the present perfect.

Today I have _____

but I haven't _____

and _____

Fan clubs

1 Find six words in the word square. They are all from Students' Book page 72.

A	T	I	C	K	E	T
A	L	T	B	R	G	L
F	J	B	O	C	N	O
A	Z	T	U	U	P	H
N	U	W	H	M	R	Y
P	O	S	T	E	R	K
V	U	Q	G	D	X	A
C	O	N	C	E	R	T

2 Write the letters from the grey boxes in Exercise 1. Order the letters and complete the sentence.

Monica

Hi, I'm famous. This is my _____!

3 Complete the text. Use words from Exercises 1 and 2.

Coldplay have made a new ¹ **album** . Ben is a great ² _____ of their music. He hasn't been to a ³ _____ yet but he's got their ⁴ _____s. They're on ⁵ _____ in Germany in July. Ben's seen the ⁶ _____ but he hasn't got a ⁷ _____ .

Present perfect with *ever / never*

4 ☆☆ Read the dialogue. Answer the questions.

Katie Mum, have you seen my new CD?

Mum No, I haven't. What is it?

Katie It's the new Norah Jones album.

Mum I've never heard of her.

Katie Oh, Mum! Have you ever heard of Ravi Shankar?

Mum Yes, of course!

Katie Well, Norah Jones is his daughter. She's really good.

Mum Has she ever been on TV?

Katie Yes. She's on Golden Disc Channel all the time but you've never watched it. I've watched it at Monica's. It's cool!

1 Has Katie's mum seen her new CD?

_____

2 Has she ever heard of Ravi Shankar?

_____

3 Has Norah Jones been on TV?

_____

4 Has Katie ever watched Golden Disc Channel?

_____

5 ☆☆ Underline the past participles of these verbs in the dialogue in Exercise 4. Circle the regular verb.

be   hear   watch   see

6 ⭐⭐ **Change the sentences into questions. Use *Have you ever* or *Has she ever*.**

1 I met a star.
   Have you ever met a star?

2 I went to a pop festival.
   _____

3 I saw my favourite singer in concert.
   _____

4 She won a prize.
   _____

5 She gave me her autograph.
   _____

6 I wrote to a famous person.
   _____

7 ⭐ **Circle the correct words.**

Henry's favourite Singer

Henry's favourite singer is Madonna but he's never ¹(met)/ **meet** her. He's never ² **see** / **seen** a famous star in person. He doesn't go to pop festivals and Madonna has never ³ **played** / **play** in his town. She's ⁴ **have** / **had** shows in New York but Henry has never ⁵ **be** / **been**. But he has got Madonna's autograph.

Yesterday was Henry's birthday and his friends ⁶ **gave** / **given** him a DVD of Madonna's concert. He hasn't ⁷ **watched** / **watch** it but he knows it's great.

Madonna's ⁸ **win** / **won** a lot of prizes and she's got a lot of fans. Some of them have ⁹ **write** / **written** to her. Henry has. He's ¹⁰ **write** / **written** to a famous person. Have you?

8 ⭐ **Imagine you are Henry. Answer the questions in Exercise 6.**
Use *Yes, I have*, *No, I haven't*, *Yes, she has* or *No, she hasn't*.

1 ***No, I haven't.***
2 _____
3 _____
4 _____
5 _____
6 _____

Present perfect and past simple

1 ⭐⭐ Write questions. Use the present perfect or the past simple.

1 you / ever / play / the trumpet
   Have you ever played the trumpet?
2 you / play / the xylophone / last year
   _____?
3 you / go / London / last summer
   _____?
4 you / ever / see / a famous pop star
   _____?
5 you / ever / be / the USA
   _____?
6 you / see / *Pop Idol* / yesterday
   _____?

2 ⭐⭐ Order the words.

a I've | of | Yes | lots | seen | pop | stars
   Yes, I've seen lots of pop stars.
b TV | No | didn't | I | watch | yesterday
   _____
c London | go | didn't | No | I | to
   _____
d too | the | I | Yes | played | guitar
   _____
e New York | been | Yes | to | I've
   _____
f instrument | never | a | played | I've
   No | musical
   _____

3 ⭐⭐ Match the sentences in Exercise 2 with the questions in Exercise 1.

1 __*f*__
2 _____
3 _____
4 _____
5 _____
6 _____

4 ⭐ Complete the sentences. Use *before* or *yesterday*.

1 This radio has never worked ***before***.
2 I saw the monkey _____ .
3 I've never been in a tree house _____ .
4 I went to the beach _____ .
5 Have you ever seen a crab _____?
6 Did you go to a concert _____?

5 Complete the dialogue. Use these words.

| never | ~~ever~~ | before | a few days |

Crab A Have you ¹ ***ever*** seen a monkey here?
Crab B No, I've ² _____ seen a monkey, but I've heard one.
Crab A When was that?
Crab B Oh, it was ³ _____ ago. Hey, listen!
Crab A What is it? I haven't heard that noise ⁴ _____!
Crab B Run!

Talking about past experiences

6 Find two questions in each box. Write them in the correct place.

~~Have~~ it ~~played~~ you ~~you~~ ~~the trumpet~~
? did **?** ~~ever~~ When play

1 *Have you ever played the trumpet?*
   Yes, I have!

2 _____
   Last year.

Danny to been a concert ever he
Has **?** before like it Did **?**

3 _____
   Yes, he has.

4 _____
   Yes, he did.

7 Complete Bonzo's poem. Use these words.

check ~~jazz~~ xylophone dog down

Bonzo's Notes

I've heard a monkey,
playing [1] *jazz*
in a tree.

I've seen a [2] _____
on a beach
by the sea.

I've travelled all over,
But this is very odd.
[3] _____ it out!
Calm [4] _____!
I'm only a [5] _____!

8 Answer the questions about the poem in Exercise 7.

1 Where did Bonzo hear the monkey?

_____

2 What did he see on the beach?

_____

3 Where has Bonzo travelled?

_____

Nipper's Learning Blog

Remember the present perfect!

Write a list of things you have to do this weekend.

clean bike

finish library book

phone Bill

buy a present for Dan

On Sunday evening tick the things you have done and write sentences.

I've cleaned my bike but I haven't …

On Tour

Reading

Tour of Light

Once again, twenty children from Uganda aged between six and eighteen have visited San Francisco. They've travelled all over the United States and won many prizes for their music and dancing. They've played to audiences in schools and theatres and the White House in Washington too. They haven't been on TV but they've made a DVD. You can see it on the Internet.

1 Read the article. True or false?

1 The children from Uganda have travelled all over the USA.   _true_
2 They have been on TV.   _____
3 They have won prizes.   _____
4 They haven't been to Washington.   _____
5 They have danced for different audiences.   _____
6 They haven't played music.   _____

2 Read the interview. Put a tick (✓) for each question in the table that is true for Amanda and for you.

Reporter Let's speak to Amanda. She went to see the show in San Francisco last night. Have you ever heard African music before?

Amanda No, never, but I've heard a lot of South American music.

Reporter Did you meet any of the children?

Amanda Yes, we did. They came to our school.

Reporter So have you made some new friends?

Amanda Yes, Stephen. He's great! He's a drummer and he's twelve. He's never been to the USA before.

Reporter Is that his autograph?

Amanda Yes, he's given me a signed photo and a DVD too!

Have you ever:

	Amanda	you
1 been to a show?	✓	
2 heard African music before?		
3 listened to South American music?		
4 met a musician or a dancer?		
5 played a musical instrument?		
6 bought an album?		

Writing

3 Use the table in Exercise 2 to write sentences about you.

1 I've _____
2 _____
3 _____
4 _____
5 _____
6 _____

2

Emergency!

My Picture Dictionary

Emergency services

1 Complete the words.

① r_e_sc_u_ e p_i_l_o_t

② f__r__ f__ght__r

③ __mb__l__nc__ __ff__c__r

④ p__l__c__ __ff__c__r

⑤ c__ __stg__ __rd

2 Circle the transport words.
Use the letters between the words to
complete the sentence.

helicopterexambulancecifireenginetipolicecarnglifeboat

Emergency service jobs are _____ !

3 What does Katie think of the jobs? Follow the lines. Write sentences.

ambulance officer — interesting
police officer — dangerous
coastguard — exciting
fire fighter — dangerous
rescue pilot — boring

1 *The ambulance officer's job is dangerous.*
2 _____
3 _____
4 _____
5 _____

my words

Do you know more words for jobs?
Write them here.

_____
_____
_____
_____

present perfect with *for / since*

1 ☆ Write the words and phrases in the correct column.

> ~~ten years~~   Friday   one o'clock
> a few minutes   half an hour   my birthday
> a long time   September   1998   three days

for	since
ten years	

2 ☆ Complete the sentences. Use *for* or *since*.

1 My family have lived in Jamaica **since** 2006.
2 It has been windy _____ ten days.
3 We haven't had a bad hurricane _____ years.
4 My dad has studied hurricanes _____ he was twelve.
5 In Australia they have used women's names for storms _____ the 19th century.
6 They have used both men and women's names for hurricanes _____ 1979.

3 ☆☆ Complete the timeline. Use these words.

> ~~a few minutes ago~~   yesterday   2003
> three hours ago   Christmas 2005   last year

```
        now
         ┼― a few minutes ago
         ┼
         ┼
         ┼
         ┼
      2002
```

Asking about past experiences

4 Read Katie's words. Write questions in the present perfect. Use *How long*.

1 'I play the piano.'
   How long have you played the piano?
2 'My sister plays basketball.'
   _____?
3 'My brother studies French.'
   _____?
4 'My mum works in a hospital.'
   _____?
5 'My grandparents live in Spain.'
   _____?

5 Look at the table. Imagine you are Katie. Answer the questions in Exercise 4.

Katie	piano	6 years
sister	basketball	last summer
brother	French	2006
mum	hospital	10 years
grandparents	Spain	a long time

1 *I've played the piano for six years.*
2 _____
   _____
3 _____
   _____
4 _____
   _____
5 _____
   _____

6 ☆ **Read the letter. Circle the correct words.**

Hi! I'm Clara

I've lived in Belize ¹(**for**)/ **since** ten years. My family have been here ² **for** / **since** 1952. We've seen a lot of changes. A lot of tourists have arrived. We've opened diving schools and organised boat trips for them.

One thing hasn't changed – the hurricanes! The worst was Hurricane Hattie in 1961. Nothing has been the same ³ **for** / **since** then. Belize City nearly disappeared! They've made a new capital city now. It's called Belmopan and it isn't in the danger zone. I haven't been there ⁴ **for** / **since** years. My brother was at school there but now he's a coastguard. He's worked on the lifeboats ⁵ **for** / **since** 2007. It's really exciting but dangerous too.

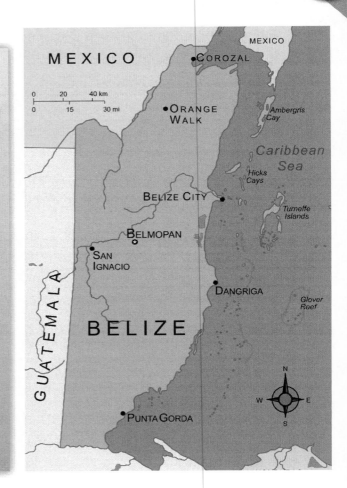

7 ☆☆☆ **Answer the questions about your town.**

1 Where do you live?

_____

2 How long have you lived there?

_____

3 Has your family always lived there?

_____

4 What changes have your family seen since 1970?

_____
_____
_____
_____
_____
_____
_____

Talking Tips!

1 Complete the dialogue. Use these words.

> rescue services   trouble   ~~wrong~~   panic

Nosy Ned	Hey! What's ¹ **_wrong_** with her?
Tall Tom	I don't know. She's in ² _____ .
Nosy Ned	Hello! Don't ³ _____!
Tall Tom	We've called the ⁴ _____!

2 Look at the pictures. Which picture do the sentences in Exercise 1 describe.

Picture _____

On the coast

3 Find seven words in the word square. They are all from Students' Book page 83.

F	A	V	E	B	E	T	H
L	S	K	B	R	I	J	S
A	W	A	V	E	S	O	P
G	T	H	N	M	A	D	A
J	N	Y	W	D	F	C	T
R	O	C	K	S	V	Q	H

4 Circle the correct words.

1 There's a red **flag** / **path** on the beach!
2 The **rocks** / **waves** are enormous today!
3 Don't jump from those **rocks** / **flags**!
4 Remember to walk on the **path** / **waves**!
5 Don't throw **cliffs** / **sand**!
6 Don't climb the **beach** / **cliffs**!

5 Complete the sentences. Use these words.

> police   ~~fire service~~   coastguard   ambulance

1
A Look! There's a fire on the mountain!
B You must call the **_fire service_**.
2
A Hey! There's a child in a boat in the sea.
B You must call the _____.
3
A Is that a person on the beach? Oh no! He's hurt!
B You must call the _____.
4
A Help! Those boys have got my bag!
B You must call the _____.

6 Match the words.

1	wear	a	careful on the beach
2	don't climb	b	after a meal
3	don't swim	c	sun cream
4	use	d	a hat
5	be	e	the cliffs

Discover **5** **extra words. Go to page 87.**

must

7 ⭐ Look at the picture and complete the sentences. Use *must* or *mustn't*.

1 The sea is dangerous! You **_mustn't_** swim today!
2 Oh no, the man's in trouble! I _____ go and help.
3 A shark! He _____ get away!
4 Hey! You _____ panic!
5 Wow, the dolphins have helped to save the man! I _____ take a photo!

8 ⭐⭐ Look at the picture and write sentences. Use *must* or *mustn't*.

Be careful on the beach!
Don't swim near a red flag.
Don't climb the cliffs.
Use sun cream.
Don't jump from the rocks.
Wear a hat.
Don't swim after a meal.

1 *You mustn't climb the cliffs.*
2 _____
3 _____
4 _____
5 _____

9 Look at the picture. Who says what? Label the sentences M (man), W (woman) or B (both).

1 You must help me! _____W_____
2 I must call the emergency services. _____
3 I mustn't stop swimming. _____
4 I mustn't panic! _____
5 I must find my phone. _____

Adventure Island

some- / any- / no-

1 ⭐ Circle the correct words.

1 Look! Nipper's got **(something)** / **anything** in his mouth!
2 Listen! There's **anyone** / **someone** coming.
3 They are going **someone** / **somewhere** safe.
4 She isn't taking **no one** / **anyone** with her.
5 She isn't saying **anything** / **something**.

2 ⭐ Complete the sentences. Use these words.

> anywhere   ~~anyone~~   someone   something
> somewhere

1 Hello! Is there **_anyone_** there?
2 I'm not going _____.
3 There's _____ in the bag.
4 Let's tell _____ the news.
5 Mum is _____ in the garden.

3 ⭐ Complete the sentences. Use *no one*, *nothing* or *nowhere*.

1 There's **_no one_** swimming today.
2 There's _____ in the box.
3 The helicopter's going _____ without a pilot.
4 I have _____ to say to you.
5 _____ told me that the cliffs were dangerous.

4 ⭐ Find the words.

1 There's (neono) **_no one_** in the sea.
2 There's (moenseo) _____ on the path.
3 There's (hgimeostn) _____ in Danny's bag.
4 They can't hear (thinyagn) _____.
5 The children are going (wmohseeer) _____.

5 Look at the pictures. Which picture do the sentences in Exercise 4 describe? _____

A

B

6 ⭐⭐⭐ Write sentences about the other picture in Exercise 5. Use *something*, *someone*, *no one* or *anywhere*.

_____

_____

_____

_____

7 Complete the words.

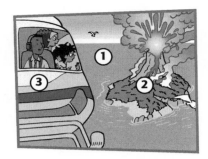

1 s_e_ _a_
2 v__ __c__ __o
3 h__l__c__pt __r
4 cr__b
5 tr__ __ h__ __s__

8 Complete Bonzo's poem. Use words from Exercise 7.

Bonzo's Notes

The ¹ _volcano_'s on fire!
There's something in the air!
I'm going to the ² _____.
I'm not staying here.

I'm looking for Nipper.
Where can he be?
He's nowhere here.
Has he gone back to the
³ _____?

There's a ⁴ _____ flying
With a rescue team.
Is there anywhere to land
That horrible machine?

Hey! There's Nipper!
Where's he been?
He's the craziest ⁵ _____
I have ever seen.

9 Read Bonzo's poem again. Answer the questions.

1 What's wrong with the volcano?
   _____

2 Where does Bonzo go?
   _____

3 Is Nipper there?
   _____

4 Are the rescue team in the helicopter?
   _____

5 Does Bonzo find Nipper?
   _____

Nipper's Learning Blog

Remember words from the unit!

Write the title of the unit in large letters. Try to find a word for each letter.

Exciting
M
E
R
Gxxxx
E
N
C
Yxxxx

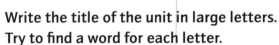

Let's Revise!

Vocabulary

1 Match the word parts to find five types of emergency transport.

> car ance boat fire cop heli en pol
> gine amb ice ul life ter

_____ _____

_____ _____

_____

2 Circle seven things you can see on the coast.

____/12

Grammar

3 Circle the correct words.

1 Children **must / mustn't** climb on the rocks.
2 Nobody **must / mustn't** play near the cliff.
3 You **must / mustn't** all be careful in the sea.
4 You **must / mustn't** read the signs on the beach.
5 Everybody **must / mustn't** wear a hat in the sun.
6 You **must / mustn't** swim after a meal.

4 Complete the table.

someone	¹ _____	no one
² _____	anything	nothing
somewhere	anywhere	³ _____

5 Complete the dialogues. Use words from the table in Exercise 4.

1 **Dora** Are you going anywhere hot?
  Serena No, I'm going _____ cold, Alaska!
2 **Danny** Is there _____ in the bottle?
  AJ No, there's _____ .
3 **Danny** Look! _____ has come to rescue us!
  AJ Hooray!

4 **Jim** Who were you with at the party?
  Dora _____ . I was alone.

6 What has Tony done today? Write sentences. Use the present perfect.

1 (go to school) _____
2 (watch TV) _____
3 (play with my dog) _____
4 (write emails) _____

7 Write sentences. Use the present perfect with *for* or *since*.

1 Jim / work / as a coastguard / six months
_____
2 Serena / be / a police officer / 1999
_____
3 Dora / be / a fire fighter / ten years
_____
4 Tara / have / a helicopter / her birthday
_____
5 They / drive / ambulances / last summer
_____

____/23

Functions

8 Write questions for the sentences in Exercise 7. Use *How long* and the present perfect.

1 _____
2 _____
3 _____
4 _____
5 _____

____/5

Your score	Your total score
	____/40

😃 31–40   🙂 21–30   ☹ 0–20

9 Friends

My Picture Dictionary

Character adjectives

1 Match the words with their opposites.

1 shy
2 hard-working
3 kind
4 silly

a lazy
b mean
c clever
d confident

2 Label the pictures. Use the words in Exercise 1.

1 _____

2 _____

3 _____

4 _____

5 _____

6 _____

7 _____

8 _____

3 Circle the correct words.

1 I don't like hard work. I'm **kind** / **lazy**.
2 He wants to be a singer. He's **confident** / **mean**.
3 They passed all the exams. They're **shy** / **clever**.
4 She didn't speak to anybody. She's **hard-working** / **shy**.
5 He pulled the cat's tail. He's **mean** / **clever**.
6 They played jokes in class. They're **kind** / **silly**.

my words

Do you know more words to describe people? Write them here.

_____
_____
_____
_____

9ᵃ No Problem!

Verb + *with / to / at / about*

1 Find the verbs. Match them with the prepositions.

1	r	e	e	a	g		*agree*
2	e	g	r	u	a		_____
3	i	l	n	t	e	s	_____
4	h	g	u	a	l		_____
5	k	a	l	t			_____
6	o	w	r	y	r		_____

at
about
with
to

2 Complete the sentences. Use these words.

with   with   ~~to~~   to   at   about

1 Talk **_to_** your teacher.
2 Listen _____ your parents!
3 Don't laugh _____ her!
4 Don't argue _____ your mum!
5 Don't worry _____ me.
6 Do you agree _____ your sister?

should

3 ☆ Complete the sentences. Use *should* or *shouldn't*.

1 You **_shouldn't_** argue with your friends.
2 You _____ always do your homework.
3 You _____ listen to your teachers.
4 You _____ copy your friend's work.
5 You _____ worry about your work.
6 You _____ ask for help!

4 ☆☆ Read about Terry's problem. Look at the graph and complete the sentences.

Hi!
My friend Judy has copied my homework.
What should I do?
Terry

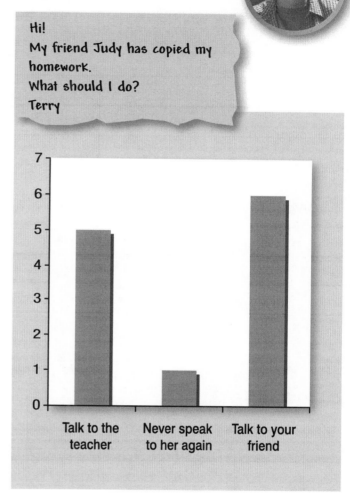

1 Five people think you should **_talk to the teacher_**.
2 One person thinks _____.
3 Six _____.

Writing

5 What do you think? Write sentences. Use *should* or *shouldn't*.

I think Terry _____

_____

6 Read the article and answer the questions.

Billy Elliot

Billy Elliot is an eleven-year-old boy. He lives in a small town in England with his dad, his older brother and his grandmother. There isn't much money in the family. Billy knows he should find a job and go to work. He knows he shouldn't buy anything silly. His dad says that Billy should start boxing lessons because a man should know how to fight. Billy doesn't like boxing. He likes dancing. He's worried about it because people laugh at him.

Billy's friends say that he shouldn't go to dancing classes. His teacher says that he shouldn't listen to his friends. He should dance!

Billy listens to his teacher.

Now, he is a famous dancer. He is in a show in London. You should go and see him! He's fantastic!

1 Why do people laugh at Billy?
They laugh at him because he likes dancing.

2 Why should Billy find a job?
_____

3 What does Billy's dad want him to learn?
_____

4 Why?
_____

5 What does Billy's teacher say?
_____

6 What does Billy do now?
_____

7 ⭐⭐ Order the words.

1 shouldn't | dance | Boys
Boys shouldn't dance.

2 shouldn't | play | Girls | football
_____

3 join | people | a | Shy | should | club
_____

4 work | shouldn't | You | school | at | too | hard
_____

5 to | Boys | how | should | box | learn
_____

6 shout | Girls | shouldn't
_____

8 Write *I agree* or *I don't agree* for each sentence in Exercise 7.

1 _____
2 _____
3 _____
4 _____
5 _____
6 _____

Talking Tips!

1 Match the words. Write four sentences.

~~Don't~~ freezing can't I'm
wait I starving ~~panic~~ I'm

1 *Don't panic!*
2 _____
3 _____
4 _____

2 Label each picture with a sentence from Exercise 1.

Ⓐ

Ⓑ

_____   _____

Present continuous for future

3 ☆☆ Order the words. Tick (✓) the sentences that are true for you.

1 meeting sister's next
  Justin Timberlake My week
  My sister's meeting Justin Timberlake next week.

2 I'm my tonight finishing project
  _____

3 My golf Saturday dad isn't on
  playing
  _____

4 We after a buying Christmas dog
  aren't
  _____

5 year I'm lessons not starting next
  piano
  _____

6 home the My in summer brother's
  leaving
  _____

4 ☆☆ What are they doing next weekend? Look at the table and write sentences in the present continuous.
Next weekend

	go bowling	meet friends	play basketball	watch DVDs
Ravi	✓	✓	✗	✓
Katie	✗	✗	✓	✗
Monica	✗	✗	✓	✓

1 Ravi / play basketball
  Ravi isn't playing basketball.
2 Ravi / meet friends
  _____
3 Katie / play basketball
  _____
4 Katie / meet friends
  _____
5 Monica / watch DVDs
  _____
6 Monica / go bowling
  _____

Discover **5** extra words. Go to page 87.

5 ⭐⭐ **Look at Ben's notebook. Complete the text. Use the present continuous for future.**

> <u>Mum and Dad's party!</u>
>
> <u>Friday</u>
> family arrive! (no cousins)
>
> <u>Saturday</u>
> barbecue
> band at 6 p.m., not cousin Annie's songs!
>
> <u>Sunday</u>
> (no football!)
> old family videos
> lunchtime - more food!
> Then presents!

Mum and Dad ¹ **_are having_** (have) a party next week. All the aunts and uncles from LA ² _____ (come) by plane on Friday. The cousins ³ _____ (not come). Too bad!

The party ⁴ _____ (start) at lunchtime on Saturday and it ⁵ _____ (finish) on Sunday night. Everybody ⁶ _____ (sleep) here!

On Saturday, we ⁷ _____ (have) a barbecue. A band ⁸ _____ (arrive) in the evening to play old songs. Cousin Annie ⁹ _____ (not sing)!

On Sunday, we ¹⁰ _____ (watch) family videos and then we ¹¹ _____ (eat) the party food from Saturday. After lunch Mum and Dad ¹² _____ (open) presents. I wonder what they'll get?

6 ⭐⭐ **Write questions about the party in Exercise 5. Add verbs in the present continuous.**

1 Ben's parents / party / next week
   Are Ben's parents having a party next week?
2 Ben's aunts and uncles / plane / Friday
   _____?

3 they / barbecue / Friday
   _____?
4 Annie / songs / Saturday evening
   _____?
5 Ben / football / Sunday
   _____?
6 Ben / presents / Sunday
   _____?

7 ⭐ **Answer the questions in Exercise 6. Use words from each cloud below.**

Yes No   he she   is isn't
               they   are aren't

1 _____
2 _____
3 _____
4 _____
5 _____
6 _____

8 **Complete the weekend diary. Think of more activities and write them on both days.**

My weekend Date:	
Saturday	**Sunday**
10 a.m.: _go bowling_	11 a.m.: _____
2 p.m.: _____	1 p.m.: _____
5 p.m.: _____	3 p.m.: _____
7 p.m.: _____	6 p.m.: _____

9 ⭐⭐⭐ **Use the diary in Exercise 8 to write sentences. Use the present continuous for future.**
I'm going bowling on Saturday morning.

_____
_____
_____
_____
_____
_____
_____

1 Complete the summary. Use these words.

> tree house   treasure   Nipper   helicopter
> volcano   rescue pilot   ~~island~~

There was something above the ¹*island* .
It was a ² _____ ! It landed on the
³ _____ .

The children ran back to the
⁴ _____ .

The ⁵ _____ said 'Please, hurry!'

They came back with Bonzo and
⁶ _____ . What about the box of
⁷ _____ ?

2 Read the text. True or false?

There are a lot of
volcanoes on the
Galapagos Islands.
We should be very
careful around
the volcanoes. We
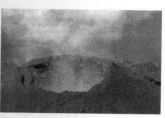
shouldn't run up to see the fire. We should stay
on the beach or in a boat.

The Galapagos Islands are full of treasure – not
jewellery, but animals and plants that we can't
find anywhere except on the islands.
We should look after the animals and plants in
the world!

1 We should be careful around volcanoes.
   true
2 We should run up to the fire to take photos.
   _____
3 We shouldn't stay on the boat.
   _____
4 We should look for jewellery on the
   Galapagos Islands. _____
5 We should look after animals and plants.
   _____

Agreeing and disagreeing

3 Circle four phrases for agreeing and disagreeing. Write them in the correct columns of the table.

No way You' I agree
tree don't agree I agree right

agreeing	disagreeing

4 Write Jan and Ali's words. Use phrases from Exercise 3.

Ali loves animals.
Jan hates islands and doesn't like animals.

1 'They shouldn't leave without Coco.'
Ali *I agree.*
Jan _____

2 'They should stay on the island.'
Jan _____

3 'They should take Bonzo.'
Ali _____

5 Complete Bonzo's poem.

| brave | ~~friends~~ | day | end |

Bonzo's Notes

They shouldn't leave
Without me.
They say they're
My ¹ *friends*
We should always stay together
Right to the ² _____.

I came back and
Rescued Nipper.
I looked for him all ³ _____.
He should always remember
That I was very ⁴ _____.

6 Read Bonzo's poem again. Answer the questions.

1 What does Bonzo think his friends shouldn't do?
_____

2 What does Bonzo think friends should always do?
_____

3 What should Nipper do?
_____

Nipper's Learning Blog

Be a teacher!

Choose a short text from the unit.
Read it aloud slowly and ask your friend to write it.
Look and tick all the words that are correct.
Write the words that are wrong with a coloured pen on a big card.
Help your friend to learn them.

Now ask your friend to choose a text for you to write.

confident

bowling alley

Film Friends

Reading

Aesop was a writer and storyteller in Greece many years ago. His stories have a lesson for life and are still famous today.

1 Read the story and answer this question.
What is the lesson of this story?
A Little friends can be great friends.
B You shouldn't play with lions.

Lioness	Are you coming for a walk this afternoon?
Lion	No way! I'm sleeping under a tree. Leave me alone.
Mouse	It's fun to run up and down on a lion's back. Oh no! Help! He's got me! Don't eat me! I can be your friend.
Lion	YOU! My friend? Ha ha ha! I doubt it.
Mouse	Please let me go. One day I can help you.
Lion	That's a funny joke. OK, then. Go away, you silly mouse.

The next day …

Mouse	Hey! That's my friend the lion. He's in a net! What can I do? I must help him.
Lion	Help! I'm in trouble.
Mouse	Don't worry. I can eat the ropes. I've got strong teeth.

Soon the lion was free …
Lion Thank you! You are a good friend!

Writing

2 The story from Exercise 1 is mixed up! Order the events. Write the letters.

a The mouse saw the poor lion in a net.
b A lion wanted to sleep under a tree.
c The lion was angry and wanted to eat the mouse.
d He ate through the net with his sharp teeth.
e The lion laughed but didn't eat him.
f A mouse wanted to have fun.
g The mouse said that a small friend can sometimes help a lion.
h The mouse ran up and down the lion's back.
i The lion was free and they were friends!

1	_b_	6	___
2	___	7	___
3	___	8	___
4	___	9	___
5	___		

3 Write the story. Use the sentences in Exercise 2. Add these words.

Then   Next day   Finally

_____
_____
_____
_____
_____
_____
_____
_____
_____
_____
_____
_____
_____

My Picture Dictionary

People in history

1 Match the word halves. Write the words.

1	phar	a	eror	1	*pharaoh*
2	qu	b	iator	2	_____
3	emp	c	aoh	3	_____
4	sol	d	een	4	_____
5	glad	e	ng	5	_____
6	ki	f	dier	6	_____

2 Match the pictures with words from Exercise 1.

A

pharaoh

B _____

C _____

D _____

E _____

F _____

3 Circle the correct words.

1 Henry VIII was a famous **pharaoh** / **king**.
2 Cleopatra was a famous **queen** / **soldier**.
3 Tutankhamen was a famous **emperor** / **pharaoh**.
4 Napoleon was a famous **king** / **emperor**.

my words

Do you know more words for people in history? Do you know any famous people in history? Write them here.

_____
_____
_____
_____

Discover 5 extra words. Go to page 87.

Periods of time

1 Order these words. Number 1 is the shortest period of time, number 10 is the longest.

> fortnight   year   week   ~~minute~~   hour
> month   day   season

1   second
2   *minute*
3   _____
4   _____
5   _____
6   _____
7   _____
8   _____
9   _____
10 century

2 Write questions.

1   How many / days / week
    How many days are there in a week?
2   How many / seconds / minute
    _____ ?
3   How many / seasons / year
    _____ ?
4   How many / days / fortnight
    _____ ?
5   How many / months / year
    _____ ?
6   How many / hours / day
    _____ ?

3 Match these numbers to the questions in Exercise 2. Write the numbers as words.

24   14   ~~7~~   12   4   60

1   *seven*   4   _____
2   _____   5   _____
3   _____   6   _____

Grammar review: units 1–5

4 ☆ Complete the table with the correct forms of the verbs.

verb	present simple	present continuous	past simple
be	I am	I am being	[1] *I was*
climb	He [2]_____	He is climbing	[3]_____
see	We [4]_____	[5]_____	We saw
have	They have	[6]_____	[7]_____
read	I [8]_____	I am reading	[9]_____
like	You [10]_____		You liked
jump	She jumps	[11]_____	[12]_____
stop	We [13]_____	We are stopping	[14]_____
save	He [15]_____	[16]_____	He saved
give	They give	[17]_____	[18]_____
go	We go	We are going	[19]_____
play	He [20]_____	He is playing	He played

5 ⭐⭐ **Complete the text. Use verbs from Exercise 4 in the correct form.**

I really ¹ *like* adventure stories. My favourite character is Spider-Man. I ² _____ my first Spider-Man film on holiday. I ³ _____ to the cinema with my mum and dad. After that, I ⁴ _____ the comics. At the moment, I ⁵ _____ my new Spider-Man comic. Now we ⁶ _____ all the DVDs in my parents' shop. My cousins ⁷ _____ me a Spider-Man video game for my birthday. It's very exciting, and I ⁸ _____ it with my friends from school. Spider-Man ⁹ _____ never boring. He ¹⁰ _____ walls and ¹¹ _____ across buildings. In *Spider-Man 2* he ¹² _____ a train! That ¹³ _____ cool. Some of his adventures ¹⁴ _____ dangerous. Spider-Man ¹⁵ _____ good people. He's a superhero!

6 ⭐⭐ **Read the text in Exercise 5 again. True or false? Correct the false sentences.**

1 Spider-Man has a lot of adventures.   *true*
2 Ravi saw his first Spider-Man film on his birthday.
_____
3 He went to the cinema with his cousins.
_____
4 He is reading a book about Spider-Man.
_____
5 In *Spider-Man 2* he stopped a train.
_____
6 Spider-Man saves bad people.
_____

7 ⭐ **Circle the correct words.**

Maurice often ¹(watches)/ watching old *Doctor Who* programmes. It's his birthday today. He ² **has / is having** a party. After the party, they ³ **are going to play / played** his new *Doctor Who* game. His sister, Marie, ⁴ **made / makes** a Dalek cake yesterday. Marie is ⁵ **old / older** than Maurice and she works in the ⁶ **more / most** expensive restaurant in town. Her friends ⁷ **help / helped** her with the cake. It hasn't got ⁸ **some / any** legs, but it's got ⁹ **a / some** chocolate body. It isn't the ¹⁰ **biggest / bigger** cake in the world but Maurice thinks it's the ¹¹ **best / better**!

8 ⭐⭐ **Look at Exercise 7. Write the words from the text or answer the questions.**

1 Write the sentence in the present continuous tense.   *He is having a party.*
2 What tense is the first sentence?
_____
3 Write the adverb in the first sentence. _____
4 Write the regular past simple verb. _____
5 Write the irregular past simple verb. _____
6 Write a comparative adjective. _____
7 Write three superlative adjectives.
_____
8 Write a sentence about the Dalek cake.
_____

Vocabulary

1 Complete the puzzle. Draw a picture of the secret word.

Crossword:
1. F O O T B A L L L (down starts B)
2. M ... Z
3. ... N
4. B
5. B
6. V ... P ... Y R
7. C H
8. P

Down: B A L Z S N B A L C P

Talking Tips!

2 Complete the dialogue. Use these words.

> sure just ~~wrong~~ trouble who
> time freezing

Kurt What's ¹ **_wrong_** with her?
Kelly ² _____ knows?
Kurt She's in ³ _____! She's ⁴ _____!
Kelly Are you ⁵ _____?
Kurt We're ⁶ _____ in ⁷ _____!

3 Read the letter. Label the pictures of Guido's favourite things.

> Hello!
> My name's Guido. We've never met. I'm from Sicily and I've lived here since 1910. My dad's a fisherman and I'm helping him this week. He's worked at sea for twenty-five years. I want to go to sea too but I have to study.
> These are my favourite things. What are yours?
> Will you write to me, please?
> Guido (age 12)

1 _____
2 _____
3 _____
4 _____
5 _____
6 _____
7 _____

4 Read Guido's letter again. Answer the questions.

1 Did Guido tell the truth?
2 How do you know? Complete the sentence.
  Because we've had _____ and _____ since 1922 but not the other things!

Grammar review: units 6–9

5 ⭐⭐ **Look at Guido's letter in Exercise 3. Find and write these things.**

1 a present perfect sentence with *for*
   He's worked at sea for twenty-five years.

2 a present perfect sentence with *since*
   _____

3 a present perfect sentence with *never*
   _____

4 two regular past participles
   _____ _____

5 an irregular past participle
   _____

6 a question in the future tense.
   _____

6 ⭐⭐ **Look at the list. Write sentences. Use _must_ or _mustn't_.**

Look! A bottle with a message
in it!

take a photo	✓
touch the bottle	✗
read the message	✗
tell your parents	✓
call the police	✓
pick it up	✗
take it home	✗

1 **_You must take a photo._**
2 _____
3 _____
4 _____
5 _____
6 _____
7 _____

7 **What do you think the children should do about the bottle?**

They should _____

They shouldn't _____

8 ⭐ **Circle the correct words.**

Hello!
You ¹ **must to** / **must** help me! The Queen
must ² **read** / **reading** this message. You
³ **must** / **mustn't** take it to her. She must
⁴ **to be** / **be** careful. We are in danger.
Everybody ⁵ **must** / **mustn't** go to the castle
and hide.

You ⁶ **must** / **mustn't** say anything to
anybody. It's a secret!

9 ⭐⭐ **Complete Ravi's email. Use the correct form of the verbs in brackets.**

Hi Monica,
Tomorrow we are visiting the castle.
I ¹ **_am taking_** (take) my camera. Yoda isn't
coming. I ² _____ (leave) him with
Ben. I ³ _____ (get up) at seven.
The bus ⁴ _____ (go) at eight. We
⁵ _____ (have) lunch in the park. I
can't wait!

What ⁶ _____ you _____ (do)
tomorrow?

Ravi

Adventure Island

10ᶜ

1 Complete the summary of the Adventure Island story. Use the names Bonzo, Nipper, Tara, Danny or AJ.

¹ _Danny_ arrives on the island with his dog,
² _____ . He meets ³ _____ and
⁴ _____ , the crab.
⁵ _____ doesn't like ⁶ _____ . He's
scared of him. ⁷ _____ is worried about
her hair.
⁸ _____ isn't very good at cooking and
⁹ _____ isn't very good at helping.
¹⁰ _____ sleeps all day.

Later they meet a girl, ¹¹ _____ .

2 Complete the story. Use these sentences.

The helicopter lands and rescues them.
The mountain is a volcano!
~~They find a map.~~
They find a radio.

The children are very excited about finding
some treasure.
They find a tree house and meet Tara.
¹ _They find a map._
They are tired of living on the island and
want to go home.
² _____
They walk up the mountain to get a signal.
³ _____
They see a helicopter flying above them.
⁴ _____
But is the treasure on the island?
Are they all happy to leave?

3 Answer the questions at the end of the story in Exercise 2.

_____
_____

4 Look at the story in Exercises 1 and 2. Answer the questions.

1 What was AJ worried about?
_____

2 What was Bonzo scared of?
_____

3 What was Danny bad at?
_____

4 What were they tired of?
_____

5 What were they excited about?
_____

6 What were they happy about?
_____

Adjective + preposition

5 ☆ Complete the sentences. Use *at*, *about* or *of*.

1 Ravi is worried **_about_** his homework.
2 Ben is tired _____ playing football.
3 Katie is good _____ history.
4 Yoda is scared _____ dogs.
5 Monica is excited _____ the concert.

6 ☆☆ Answer the questions for you.

1 What are you good at?
_____

2 What are you bad at?
_____

3 What are you excited about?
_____

4 What are you worried about?
_____

5 What are you scared of?
_____

Talking about your feelings

7 Look at the table. Write sentences about Adventure Island.

Nipper Bonzo Danny AJ Tara	is isn't	going to miss	swimming. eating fish. going to school.
		looking forward to	living in a tree house. watching TV. looking for treasure. going shopping. sleeping in a bed.
	can't wait to		see his / her friends. wash his / her hair. go to a party.

1 *AJ isn't going to miss eating fish.*
2 _____
3 _____
4 _____
5 _____
6 _____
7 _____

8 Imagine you are going to live on Adventure Island with your family for a month. Complete the sentences.

I'm going to miss _____
_____

I can't wait to _____
_____

I'm looking forward to _____
_____

9 Match the rhyming words.

tree   sure
too   me
more   you

10 Use four of the words in Exercise 9 to complete Bonzo's poem.

Bonzo's Notes

Am I happy about leaving?
I'm not really ¹ _____ .
I've made some new friends.
I won't see them any ² _____ !
I'm sad about that,
But I'm tired of Nipper ³ _____ .

I'm going to miss AJ,
The island and ⁴ _____ !

Nipper's Learning Blog

Make a quiz!

Work with your friends.
Choose a unit from the book.
Prepare a quiz about the unit.
Each person chooses a page from the unit and writes questions.
The quiz can have ten questions.
Put in some spelling questions too!

QUIZ

1 Write the opposite of shy.

Vocabulary

1 Find six people in history and four periods of time in the word square.

Y	E	M	P	E	R	O	R	Q
E	M	Y	H	K	D	L	G	U
A	O	V	A	C	I	P	N	E
R	N	I	R	J	O	N	U	E
A	T	R	A	Y	S	X	G	N
Z	H	S	O	L	D	I	E	R
O	W	F	H	D	A	Y	M	S
G	L	A	D	I	A	T	O	R
Q	W	E	E	K	S	E	M	H

2 Complete. Use words from Exercise 1.

1 _____ Elizabeth was a famous ruler of England.
2 _____ Henry VIII had six wives.
3 _____ were the rulers of Egypt.
4 There were _____ and _____ in Rome many years ago.
5 The _____ marched outside the palace.

___/16

Grammar

3 Match the sentence halves.

1 He's scared   **a** at maths.
2 Are you tired   **b** of spiders.
3 She is excited   **c** at English?
4 Are you good   **d** about her birthday.
5 My sister's bad   **e** of eating pizza every day?

4 Circle the correct words.

1 We're **going** / **go** on holiday tomorrow!
2 I **must** / **must to** pack my rucksack.
3 I'm **miss** / **going to miss** my favourite TV programme tonight.
4 You should **watch** / **watched** the DVD.

5 Have you got **one** / **any** good photos?
6 I've never **seen** / **saw** a Dalek.
7 The dog **find** / **found** a box of treasure.

5 Order the words. Write the questions.

1 you | What | time | capsule | a | in | mustn't | put
_____?

2 Spider-Man | seen | Have | a | ever | film | you
_____?

3 ever | in | been | tree | house | Have | you | a
_____?

6 Complete.

1 There are _____ _____ in a fortnight.
2 There are _____ _____ in a year.
3 There are _____ _____ in a minute

___/18

Functions

7 The children are going to a new class. Complete the sentences. Use *miss*, *can't wait* or *looking forward*.

1 I'm going to _____ my teacher!
2 I _____ to start French lessons.
3 I'm _____ to wearing my new trainers.
4 I am going to _____ my English book!
5 I _____ to meet new friends.
6 I'm _____ to studying new things.

___/6

Your score	Your total score
	___/40

31–40   21–30   0–20

Unit 1 Find the words.

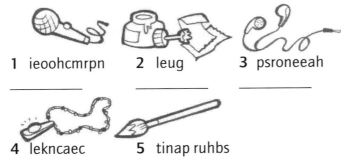

1 ieoohcmrpn _____ 2 leug _____ 3 psroneeah _____

4 lekncaec _____ 5 tinap ruhbs _____

Unit 2 Complete the sentences.

There's some water in the ¹ _j___g_ and some milk in the ² _b__t_t_l___ . There's a ³ _s_l___c__ of cake on the ⁴ _t_r___y_ . There aren't any plates but you can have a ⁵ _n___p_k___n_ !

Unit 3 Circle the correct words.

1 There was a very long **shop assistant** / **queue**.
2 The **shelf** / **shop assistant** was not happy.
3 The **till** / **shelf** was open.
4 The money was on the **queue** / **counter**.
5 The mystery books were on the **shelf** / **queue**.

Unit 4 Complete the sentences. Use these words.

> trucks   bush   pavement   wheel   skyscrapers

1 The London Eye is a big _____ .
2 There's a green _____ in the garden.
3 The _____ are noisy and dirty.
4 All big cities have got tall _____ .
5 They are standing on the _____ .

Unit 5 Find the words.

ˢᵗᵃˡᵏᵗʳᵘⁿᵏᵇʳᵃⁿᶜʰᵈᵉᵉʳˡᵉᵃᶠ

Unit 6 Match the words. Complete words 4 and 5 with the circled letters.

1 washing   a pa(n)   4 __ _i_ __ _k_
2 (s)hoe   b (p)olish   5 _t_ __ __ __
3 frying   c m(a)chine

Unit 7 Find the words.

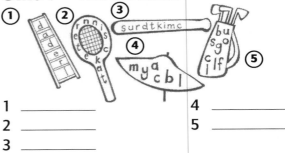

1 _____   4 _____
2 _____   5 _____
3 _____

Unit 8 Circle the correct words.

1 You must wear a **helmet** / **stretcher** on a bike.
2 I can hear a **lifejacket** / **siren**. What's wrong?
3 Dial the **siren** / **number** for emergency services.
4 We wear a **lifejacket** / **stretcher** on a boat.
5 The ambulance officers carried the person on a **stretcher** / **helmet**.

Unit 9 Complete the words.

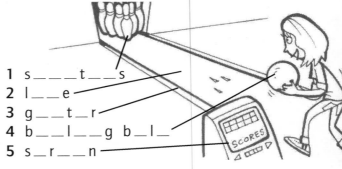

1 s_ _ _ _t_ _ _s
2 l_ _ _e
3 g_ _ _t_ _r
4 b_ _ _l_ _ _g b_ _l_ _
5 s_ _r_ _ _n

Unit 10 Complete the puzzle. Find the secret word.

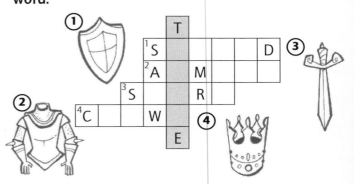